Training For Trail Horse Classes

LAURIE TRUSKAUSKAS

Alpine
PUBLICATIONS
Loveland, Colorado

Training For Trail Horse Classes

Library of Congress Cataloging-in-Publication Data

Truskauskas, Laurie, 1957-
    Training for trail horse classes / Laurie Truskauskas.
      p. cm.
    ISBN 1-57779-036-7
     1. Trail horse class. 2. Horses--Training. I. Title

SF296.T7 T78 2001
798.2'3-- dc21

2001046430

This book is available at special quantity discounts for club promotions, premiums, or educational use. Write for details.

The information contained in this book is complete and accurate to the best of our knowledge. All recommendations are made without guarantee on the part of the author or Alpine Publications, Inc. The author and publisher disclaim any liability with the use of this information.

Cover and text design: Laura Claassen
Photography: Gary Sperber
Illustrations: Elizabeth Marshall

First printing March 2002

1 2 3 4 5 6 7 8 9 0

Printed in the United States of America.

TABLE OF CONTENTS

DEDICATION

To
Betty McKinney and the staff at Alpine Publications
who make masterpieces
out of the tangled mess of words that I send
with the accompanying stacks of photographs.
The more I write, the more I appreciate the people
who put it all together into book form.

INTRODUCTION

A well-trained trail horse is truly a joy to ride. A good trail horse will allow you to cue him step-by-step on obstacles that require it, while he'll practically negotiate other obstacles by himself. The key to training a successful trail horse is to start slowly and teach your horse to obey the cues to maneuver through an obstacle, rather than let the horse anticipate and perform the *pattern* of an obstacle—or perform an obstacle by habit. Anticipation can cost you points in tough competition.

Horses enjoy the challenge of working different obstacles. The skills and knowledge they gain from learning one maneuver or obstacle helps when you progress to the next. The discipline of maneuvering correctly through the obstacles will teach your horse obedience and to be more respectful, which in turn will make him a more enjoyable partner. The obstacles add variety and "spice" to a horse's life. Changing the pattern of the obstacles adds variety and will provide both you and your horse countless hours of enjoyment. The new challenges of a demanding trail course can help an otherwise bored horse become competitive once again.

The trail obstacles also give the rider a visual aid to see if they have correctly cued their horse. This will help you fine tune your cues to the horse, making you a more polished rider. Rider error can cause the best trained horse to make a mistake. In many cases, the horse is doing exactly what the rider cued him to do. For example, if you use too strong a leg cue when turning in reverse in an "L" back-up, your horse may step out over the poles or bump a pole, both points off your maneuver, and both rider error.

When you have completed the training program outlined in this book, you'll have the ability to move your horse's head, hips, and shoulders on cue, which will enable you to successfully negotiate any obstacles that you'll find in a trail class, even if you've never encountered a similar obstacle before. Once you've developed a solid working relationship with your horse, he or she will hold a special place in your heart for many years to come.

ACKNOWLEDGMENTS

I would like to thank Joe Ferro, who started me on the path to thinking that "what you teach a horse today, he learns tomorrow." I've fine-tuned what I learned from him and hopefully can pass on our many years of combined experience.

I am indebted, also, to all the horses that I have trained over the years and to their owners who allowed me to put into practice what I've learned. Experiences with them form the basis for this book.

And a special "thank you" to the people of Athens, Texas and surrounding areas who have made me feel welcome, proving this move to be the right one.

FOREWORD

Good trail class skills don't just happen. Before a rider can experience the feeling of victory that comes from being able to complete a trail class successfully or finish a pattern with no penalties, they need to put in long hours of hard work.

Laurie Truskauskas is a trainer, teacher, and top competitor who recognizes that fact. It is the reason she wrote *Training for Trail Horse Classes*. If you ever competed in a trail riding class then you know there is no greater joy than riding a well-mannered, highly trained horse through a series of obstacles. How to get yourself and your horse to this point is the focus of this book.

Through *Training for Trail Horse Classes*, riders at all levels can improve their skills and their horse's confidence. The book is written in an "explain then ride" method with instructions that are easy to understand and apply. Complete, illustrated directions help you quickly understand and show you how to apply each technique in the ring or on the trail. For beginners, this book is basic and simple to understand, yet at the same time it offers insights that intermediate and advanced riders can appreciate. She includes exercises to build specific riding skills and improve communication between you and your horse. Each chapter has step-by-step lessons and tips for better performance. A large majority of the book provides techniques for training on trail obstacles. She also provides leg and reining techniques.

Training for Trail Horse Classes focuses on teaching you what you must know in order to ride correctly when your horse faces a complex task, such as crossing a bridge or backing through an obstacle. Throughout the book, Laurie stresses good position, balance, and use of aids. These techniques can improve any rider's performance. A must read for anyone whose goal is to become a better rider, whether on the trail or in the ring!

Dawn Sekel
Editor, *Horse Daily Planner Publications*

Photo © Larry Larson.

ONE

INTRODUCTION TO TRAIL

THE TRAIL CLASS is judged on a horse's ability to successfully negotiate obstacles of various degrees of difficulty. The horse is judged on his performance and ability over the obstacles as well as on his attitude, his manners, and his response to the rider. An eye catching horse with an alert, pleasant expression that negotiates the obstacles cleanly, with a slight degree of speed when possible, will do well in this class.

At the larger breed shows, trail classes may be broken down into junior and senior divisions based on the horse's age. A junior trail horse is five years old and younger, while a senior horse is six years old and over. When the class is broken down in this way, the obstacles in the junior class are not as demanding as the obstacles used for the senior horse. This makes it possible for the young horse to gain experience while competing against horses of the same age.

At 4-H shows and local shows, the classes are broken down according to the rider's age. Again, the courses for the younger riders are easier and less demanding. The degree of difficulty increases as the age of the rider increases. Trail is a great class for kids

Riders of all ages compete in trail classes.

Youth classes are usually divided according to the age of the riders. This little guy is contemplating the time when he can compete.

that may not have the best moving or best looking horse. A horse that is well-mannered, quiet, and easily obeys the rider's cues can win on those qualities alone in trail class.

For all riders, training for trail class is a great way to sharpen your skills and fine-tune your cues to your horse. You will learn to use your hand and leg aids to put the horse in the correct position to maneuver through the obstacles, and your horse will learn many practical skills that will make him more pleasurable and versatile.

THE IDEAL TRAIL HORSE

A horse that is not easily ruffled is an asset in this class. He should readily perform new and varied maneuvers. Look for a horse that naturally and carefully picks his way over or through different terrain or obstacles such as poles on the ground.

You can partially evaluate a horse as he moves about in the pasture or

This filly and her dam check out some trail obstacles. Will she be a future trail class horse? Only time will tell.

down the trail. Does he panic or spook every time something is out of place or has changed? If he must pick his way through logs on the ground, does he do it readily? Or does he panic and fret? A panicky horse is not suited to trail. Look for a horse that responds to soft and light leg and rein cues. The trail class obstacles and maneuvers can be taught to any horse, but it is easiest to start with one that naturally has the qualities to excel in your chosen discipline, especially if your goal is to own the next World Champion Trail Horse.

THE OBSTACLES

Most breed associations have a list of required obstacles and a list of optional obstacles. The specific lists can be found in their rule book. The required obstacles must be included in every trail course. The optional obstacles are used to fulfill the requirement for the minimum number of obstacles required for each course. These optional obstacles are chosen at the judge's or at the show committee's discretion. Many of the obstacles are discussed in this book, but feel free to add variety to your practice sessions to prepare your horse for whatever he may find at a show. Look at the obstacles at a show and try to recreate them, or a variation of them, at home. Be sure the obstacles you use are safe so that neither you nor your horse can get hurt. Don't scare your horse by asking him to perform an obstacle that is beyond his ability at any point in time. Training takes time.

The American Quarter Horse Association and the American Paint Horse Association no longer require a horse to go back in the ring to walk, jog, and lope on the rail when they have finished performing the obstacles.

THE AMERICAN QUARTER HORSE ASSOCIATION RULE BOOK

To give you a general idea of what you might find in a trail class, the required obstacles in the Quarter Horse Association rule book are:

∩ **Opening, passing through, and closing a gate.**

∩ **Ride over at least four logs or poles set in a straight, curved, or zig zag line. These may be either a walk-over, trot-over, or lope-over set at the correct distance for each.**

∩ **A backing obstacle—U, V, L, or around three cones, as designated by the pattern.**

∩ **The optional obstacles can include maneuvers such as side passing, the mail box, a water box, or any other obstacle that might reasonably be found on a trail.**

THE AMERICAN PAINT HORSE ASSOCIATION

The American Paint Horse Association rules require a minimum of six obstacles and a maximum of eight obstacles, with two obstacles being chosen from each division— A through D.

∩ **Division A requires that your horse jump an obstacle not less then fourteen inches nor more than twenty-four inches or cross four poles in a walk-over, jog-over, or lope-over.**

∩ **Division B includes a sidepass, a circle, a square, or a gate.**

∩ **Division C includes a back through, a bridge, or a water hazard.**

∩ **Division D requires a slicker, a mail box, carry an object, jog-through or around poles, or a serpentine pattern.**

The required obstacles can include a gate . . .

. . . and crossing a series of poles . . .

. . . a back-up between poles.

However, the three gaits are required somewhere between obstacles and are considered as part of the maneuver score.

Your horse does not have to be a great moving horse to win at trail if he performs the obstacles with brilliance and distinction, but you must still work on getting the best quality of gait between the obstacles. It may mean the difference between first and second place, or the last placed ribbon and the gate. Quality and cadence of gaits are discussed elsewhere in this book. Be sure your horse will depart promptly into each gait.

HOW CLASSES ARE JUDGED

Each obstacle is scored independently of the others on the pattern. This means that if your horse refuses to cross the bridge, for example, that he is not automatically eliminated from the class. He just receives a no score for the obstacle. He will place lower than another horse that negotiates every obstacle correctly, but he may place higher than a horse that has a poor showing at two or more of the obstacles. Always continue to show your horse to the best of your ability, even if you have problems at one (or more) of the obstacles. The class isn't over until it is over, and you never know how the other competitor's horses will fare.

The horse that wins the trail class is one that negotiates each obstacle with skill and finesse. A horse that completes an obstacle with a slight degree of speed but does not sacrifice the quality of maneuvering through the obstacle will be scored higher than a horse that completes the same obstacle at a slower pace. This does not mean that a trail class is a timed event—it is not. However, if a horse

A good trail horse is alert and looks where he is placing his feet.

completes an obstacle cleanly with a slight degree of speed, it shows his understanding of the obstacle and his willingness to quickly obey his rider's cue, and he will earn a higher score.

The judge is looking for a horse that shows interest in his surroundings, not a dull or intimidated horse. Your horse cannot stumble blindly over an obstacle. He must look where he is going. Be sure to allow him to drop his head to look where he is placing his feet. Look for a horse that shows a natural talent in picking his way carefully over varied terrain. The qualities to look for in a prospective trail horse are discussed in more detail in the next chapter.

At larger shows especially, the quality and cadence of gaits are judged. Photo © BJ McKinney

TRAINING FOR TRAIL

Training for trail requires that you develop such control over the horse that you can move his front and rear legs, head, and shoulders, on cue. Before teaching the actual obstacles, you must teach your horse to obey leg and rein cues. Leg pressure used in one manner may mean to side pass. When used in a slightly different manner, it may mean to move his hip around the corner in a back-up obstacle. The skill and finesse obtained through this training will give you many hours of satisfaction as you find

A well-trained trail horse is a joy to ride. Queenie is counter-bending.

visual aid of the obstacles, that is, poles and cones to go around or through, you will know when you are putting your horse exactly where you want him. If you over-cue, your horse may step out of or bump the obstacles. If you under-cue, your horse may not make the desired move. As you practice, you'll learn exactly how much pressure it takes to make your horse perform a maneuver correctly. The obstacles that once were difficult will become easier over time.

Training for trail is fun, plus it will improve your horse in many ways. Teaching the trail obstacles enforce obedience, and that alone will make your horse a more enjoyable partner. You will feel a great sense of satisfaction the first time your horse backs through an "L" or crosses his first bridge. The obstacles give you a visual aid to see if you have maneuvered your horse to the correct spot, and this will help you to be a better rider. Plus, you can show your friends your horse's ability, whether it is opening and closing a gate, side passing over a pole, or allowing you to get the mail without dismounting.

You can use the trail obstacles as a test of your skills, even without an instructor to critique you. Break each obstacle down into steps and use those steps as a weekly goal to accomplish. For example, the first week, your goal is to back out between two poles. The second week, you can add two more poles to make an "L" back-up. You can tighten the distance between poles on the third week.

Training a horse for trail is more than just getting ready for a show ring class. You are teaching your horse to obey your aids with a whisper of a cue, and to move his head, hips, and shoulders on command. You can teach him to negotiate obstacles. Even if you never show your horse, you will still

out how truly maneuverable a horse can be. The training that you do for trail classes will help in many situations, not just over the obstacles. Even if your goal is not to win a trail class, a fine-tuned trail horse is a joy to ride, and teaching the skills needed is half the fun.

Practicing the trail obstacles at home will add variety to your horse's work schedule. It will help to prevent the boredom that comes after riding round and round the arena. Your horse will enjoy the change of pace and will become more responsive in other areas. Because you have the

Even if you never show your horse, you can have hours of fun practicing the trail obstacles and your horse will learn many practical skills.

For example, how many times have you wished your horse would stand quietly while you put on a coat or rain slicker? After you've learned these trail class lessons, you can even pick your slicker off the fence and safely put it on without dismounting.

have hours of fun practicing and a great sense of satisfaction from all that you have taught your horse, and it will make him a safer horse to ride on real trails, too.

SUCCESS THROUGH TRAINING

In the following chapters, I will give you exercises to start your horse on a successful trail horse career. Take this program one step at a time and build on what your horse has previously learned so that you keep him calm, confident, and willing. Patience is absolutely essential when training. Most horses truly want to please. Many problems begin because the rider does not allow the horse time to understand what it is that he is being asked to do. Remember, a small step today becomes a big step tomorrow and three steps on the following day. Your horse will learn according to his time schedule—not yours. If you listen closely, your horse will tell you when he is ready to take the next step. It is my hope that this book will help you learn to "think like a horse" and talk to a horse in a language that he can understand.

Here the horse is entering a box in a class. He will be required to execute a turn inside the box without stepping outside the poles.

Two

CHOOSING A
TRAIL HORSE

IF YOU PLAN to buy a horse specifically for trail, certain requirements apply whether the prospect is young or old, broke or unbroken. Starting with a horse that is good-minded, trainable, quiet, and that places his feet carefully will make your job as a trainer easier. Watch a horse at play to gain some insight into his natural ability. Is he graceful or clumsy? Does he look where he puts his feet or does he just plunk them down anywhere? Will he step cleanly over a pole or does he rap it with a hoof? Put him in a round pen and watch him jog and lope to see how he moves. Does he move flat off his shoulder or does he have a lot of knee action? Do his hocks move straight forward or do they wobble from side to side as he travels? Does he move slow-legged or quickly in a pitter-patter manner? Does he track in a straight line, neither toeing in or out excessively? Does he float or hit the ground with a thud? Does he have that certain presence about him that makes you want to look at him? The closer to ideal he is now as raw material (whether or not he is broke to ride), the easier it will be to "make" the finished product—a horse that is a joy to ride and one that everyone wants to own.

SEARCHING FOR THE PERFECT TRAIL HORSE

While I can give you basic guidelines to finding a good, prospective trail horse, the final decision is yours. Look beyond pretty. And color. Both are a bonus—if the horse otherwise fits the bill. Trainability, agility, and athletic ability are very important.

A good-moving horse looks as if he is floating across the ground.

This two-year-old has the quiet, willing attitude so necessary for trail.

Look for natural ability and rate.

Consider all factors before making a purchase. You also need to decide if this horse will be shown to a World level or at a local, state, or 4-H level. There is a difference in the quality of horse needed.

When you look for a prospect, take his age into account. A two-year-old that has been ridden for only a few weeks will not have the same polish as an older horse. If you look at a horse that is not saddle broke, watch the way he moves. His natural talent should show through when he is

unencumbered by a rider. That will not change as he matures (unless his feet are neglected). A good prospective trail horse will show his inherent ability at a young age. Watch his walk, jog, and lope. Ask him to go over poles to see how he handles his feet. Does he crash through or place his feet carefully? Watch his expression when being handled. Is he alert and pleasant or resistant and sour? These are all clues that can give you insight to this horse's suitability as a trail horse.

Agility is another requirement. A horse that requires a lot of room to maneuver will not handle a tight course as well as a more agile horse. If you have the opportunity to ride several horses, compare them. Notice that what one horse handles with ease, another cannot possibly perform because he lacks agility and the ability to maneuver in tight spaces. The right horse must show a certain amount of willingness and maneuverability. Not all horses are suited to be shown in trail class, just as not all horses are suited to be jumpers or reiners or pleasure horses.

A horse that has a lot of natural rate is a bonus. He will naturally enter a jog-over or lope-over and meet the poles in stride. A horse that can adjust the length of his stride to match the width of the poles in a trot-over or lope-over can save you months of training. Some horses will rate naturally; others learn it in time. A few never seem to get the idea. A horse that has the ability to determine the easiest and best way to get through an obstacle is a blessing. The less maneuvering or guiding you have to do, the better. A horse that stays calm under pressure is one that you will appreciate more and more as the courses get tougher and tougher.

Some horses' way of going can be enhanced by proper shoeing (especially if the horse's feet are out of

You can add trail to your western riding or reining horse.

shape). Ask your farrier for a pre-purchase exam just as you would a vet, and offer to pay him. Be sure your farrier is experienced with the breed and type of horse that you show. Some horses that could be good movers are unable to do so because their hooves are too long, their hoof angles don't match, or their heels are too short. Have your horse trimmed or shod by a farrier who is qualified to shoe your type of horse. Ask your vet for his opinion or pay a trainer to watch your horse move if you are unsure.

If a horse is quiet on trails, the transition to trail classes should be easy.

ADDING TRAIL TO YOUR PLEASURE HORSE'S ROUTINE

Trail is a nice class to add to your pleasure horse's routine, if he has the ability needed to compete over obstacles. It breaks up the routine of going around the rail at a walk, jog and lope, which may help his attitude if he has become bored or sour with rail work. Teaching him cues to move the various parts of his body will enable you to ride more with your legs and seat and less with hand movements that draw attention to the fact that you are cueing or correcting your horse.

Training for trail can be added to your performance horse's routine to break up the monotony. Look for the qualities outlined above no matter how the horse is currently being used. Even if you don't show in trail, the training is fun and it will help your horse become more flexible, safe, and enjoyable to ride.

An attractive horse can help draw a judge's attention.

Remember, color is a bonus, after trainability and movement.

FINDING THOSE WINNING TOUCHES

If you are looking for a horse to show at the higher levels, look for a horse with an eye-catching presence and a pretty way of going. He should be quiet and tractable. He should move with very little or no knee action and reach underneath himself with his hind legs, pushing himself forward rather than letting his front legs pull him. His hind feet should come close to, but not strike, his front feet. The horse should cover ground easily, making it look effortless. Go to a few shows and study the horses in a trail class. Watch how they move. A good moving horse should be balanced, agile, and move forward easily, maintaining the cadence of a two-beat jog and three-beat lope.

When choosing a prospect, something about the horse should draw your attention to him. Is it the way he moves, his looks, or his charisma? Color is a

A nice looking palomino.

bonus. Something about the horse must make the judge take a second look. An extremely soft and well-trained horse will always catch a judge's eye—so the basis lies in the horse's training. If two horses are equally well-trained and perform the obstacles with the same degree of finesse, however, the horse's way of going or eye-catching charisma can become the determining factor. You can enhance a horse's appearance with a well-fitting tack and by wearing clothing that matches or complements your horse's color. But, it is the way the horse performs that the judge will notice first and foremost. With that thought in mind, find a horse that is trainable and retains what he is taught.

Searching for the perfect horse is often frustrating, sometimes enlightening, and usually involves looking at a large number of horses until you find the horse that suits you. That horse can lope the "T," sidepass the "W" and back through the "L" and

still come out smelling like the daisies in the flower pots in the "U" shaped back-up. Do not give up. He is out there. He may already be in your back yard!

REQUIREMENTS OF A TRAIL HORSE

- ∩ **Careful where he places his feet**
- ∩ **A good mind; willing and trainable**
- ∩ **Natural ability over obstacles**
- ∩ **Calm disposition under pressure and when in strange surroundings**
- ∩ **Balanced, agile movement**
- ∩ **Presence that makes him stand out.**

Something about a top trail prospect should attract your—and therefore a judge's—attention.

THREE

COUNTER-BENDING

THE BASIC TRAINING for a competitive trail horse is the same as for any performance event—you must develop flexibility, willingness and smoothness of motion. The counter-bend is a training exercise. You will not be asked to do it at a show. You can begin teaching these exercises within a few weeks of breaking a colt to saddle, or you can start with a horse of any age. I use the counter-bend to teach a horse to obey leg pressure. Applying leg pressure with your inside leg and bending the horse around it lays the basis for teaching a horse to move away, and to counter-bend. Cones provide a visual aid so that you can determine whether or not the horse is going where you directed him. A twenty-year-old horse is still basically "green broke" if he doesn't understand the concept of yielding to leg pressure or giving to the bit.

LEARN A SIMPLE EXERCISE WITH MAXIMUM BENEFITS

Set up six cones in your arena, spaced about twenty feet apart. Spend a few minutes the first couple of days walking in and out of the cones in a series of half circles, first left and then right in a serpentine pattern. When the horse grasps the concept of following his nose and bending around your leg (usually within a few days to a week), begin to jog between the cones in the same pattern. Do not over-do this at first. A few minutes through this pattern, followed by five to ten minutes of rail or other work before coming back to repeat the serpentine pattern is a good plan to start. You do not want to bore your horse. He should meet the center point between the two cones and make a consistently round half-circle to get from one center point between cones to the next center point. That is your goal.

Following this pattern will teach a horse to turn both left and right and follow his nose. The cones make it easy for the horse to understand the sequence of left and right. Because you use first one rein to turn left, and then the other rein to turn right, the horse learns to give to bit pressure on first one side and then on the other. There is no solid hold on his mouth that he can set against and pull and/or "walk through the reins." Teaching the horse to give to pressure first on one side of his mouth and then the other side will allow you to later teach him to give to pressure on both sides of his mouth. When the time

1. Spend the first few days serpentining the cones at a walk.

2. This exercise first teaches your horse to "follow his nose."

3. Later, it helps him to understand that he is to move away from leg pressure cues. My inside leg pushes him away from the cone while my reins keep a slight bend in his neck.

comes to ask him to flex at the poll as he travels in a straight line, he will more readily understand what you want. This concept is similar to trying to force a balky horse that has planted his feet on the ground to go straight forward. You cannot pull him forward, but if you pull him to one side or the other, you can make him move. Similarly, when you ride and turn a horse first to the left and then to the right, he begins to learn the cues that make him soften his jaw (or give to the bit) and move first in one direction

and then in the other. Eventually, he will come to understand what you want when you apply rein pressure on both reins, asking him soften his jaw and flex at the poll while walking in a straight line. Applying an inside leg to bend your horse as you maneuver through the cones will teach him to move away from leg pressure. It will also help him to understand that legs mean more than just "go." Almost any horse can become soft, supple, and maneuverable if brought back to basics and trained to the correct use of

A properly adjusted snaffle bit and running martingale on a young horse.

the aids. Although it is easier to teach a horse correctly from the beginning, you can teach an older horse, too. It just takes longer.

BEGIN THE EXERCISE

First outfit your young horse in a snaffle, your older horse in his customary bit, and add a running martingale to your equipment. The running martingale will help to keep the horse's head in the proper position. It will prevent him from raising his head to evade bit pressure. When training, always try to make it easy for the horse to learn the correct response.

I start in the arena because the ground is flat and free of obstacles, but any open, flat area free of obstacles, such as a section of pasture, will work. Working a horse outside the confines of the arena can help to teach him that he must obey under all circumstances, not just when he is confined by the fence of your arena.

An older horse in a shank bit. She flexes at the poll nicely, bends correctly, and follows her nose.

Ride at a walk with a rein in each hand. Take the left rein in your left hand and ask the horse to make a left half-circle around the cone on your left. At the same time, apply a left leg cue at the girth and ask your horse to bend around your leg as you turn him. Be sure to bring your left hand up towards the top of your left hip. To allow the horse to bend his head correctly, you must move your right hand

This mare's hind leg has crossed over. It will be followed by the right front with her next step.

Bend around the cones. Here, Splash is resisting the rein cue and not bending as he should, so I'll continue to ask for the bend until I get it—even if I circle the cone.

forward so his head has the freedom of movement to bend into the circle. Think of bicycle handle bars. When one hand moves back, the other must move forward. The same is true of riding. You must allow a horse room to turn his head in the direction of the bending rein by loosening the outside rein—although you can lay that rein across his neck as an additional neck rein cue. Unless you release the outside rein, your horse may begin to fight the bit or toss his head to evade the conflicting bit pressure.

You must bring your inside, bending hand to the top of your hip, (or even above) to teach the horse to keep his inside shoulder up. Dropping your hand below your hip will force your horse to drop his shoulder, the exact opposite of what you want. As you lift your inside rein, the ideal response is for the horse to bend his neck into the turn, slightly flex at the poll and "give" to the bit. The rein should feel "soft" and "giving" in your hand. It should not feel as if the horse is pulling on you or that you are pulling the horse around the circle. His jaw should feel soft and relaxed as he bends into the circle. That feeling should transmit through your reins to your hand. That is the goal towards which you must work.

Your horse probably will not accomplish this immediately. Plan to spend two to three weeks serpentining through the cones until your horse learns to arc his body around your inside leg (from leg pressure applied at the girth) and follow his nose. Your leg creates the same arc in his spine as the half circle around the cones. Push with your inside leg to make him arc his body. He must move his rib cage to the outside, away from the pressure.

He must learn that your leg cue means to move away from pressure. This is the beginning of leg pressure training.

LOOK WHERE YOU ARE GOING

Be sure to look where you are going! When you look in the direction that you are asking the horse to turn, and justify your shoulder, and rein hand (left in this example) move backward, asking for the bend. Your right shoulder moves forward, almost automatically giving the horse enough outside rein to make the turn. Your left hip moves back, almost putting your left leg in the correct position and your right hip moves forward. In time your horse will read these signals as a cue to move to the left, and vice versa. If you always look where you are going and allow your body to make those subtle changes, your horse will learn to read what your body is saying even without the benefit of the rein aid. However, if you look to the right and ask the horse to turn to the left, you will give conflicting signals.

Be sure to always lift your rein to keep your horse upright and balanced between the reins and to keep him from dropping a shoulder. If a horse correctly bends his head and neck into the circle, he will be unable to drop his shoulder. This is the reason for teaching him to follow his nose and bend correctly.

In the initial stages of training, you may need to exaggerate your aids. This is perfectly acceptable. As your horse gains understanding of this, or

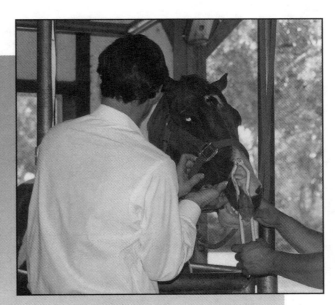

CHECK FOR WOLF TEETH

If your horse raises his head in the air, gaps his mouth, or otherwise shows resistance in his mouth, it may be a physical problem rather than a training problem. You must first solve the physical problem before you can address the training problem. If your horse fights your signals from the bit by excessively opening his mouth, have his teeth checked by a qualified equine vet or dentist. He might have sharp edges on his teeth, abscesses in his mouth, or any other number of abnormalities that a good equine vet can locate and correct. A young horse can have caps or he may have wolf teeth, (small pointed pre-molars that sit in front of his molars or grinding teeth) which can interfere with the bit and cause pain. You wouldn't go to work with a splitting toothache and put in a top performance. How can you expect your horse to?

1. This more advanced horse is soft and light. If you pull with one hand, the left in this example, you must release some rein on the opposite side.

2. Be sure to bring your hand up to keep the horse's shoulders up.

3. Cueing this way is wrong. It will teach a horse to drop his shoulders.

of any new maneuver, begin to lighten up or refine your aids. The goal of all training is to teach the horse that he gains relief from pressure when he responds correctly.

USING THE SERPENTINE

At the exact center between the cones, when changing from a left-hand half-circle to a right-hand half-circle, you must switch your aids. The easiest way to remember which hand and leg to use is to always use the hand and leg next to the cone. For example, when making a right half-circle, use your inside (right) hand and inside (right) leg. As you cross the center line to make a left circle, switch to the left inside rein and a left inside leg. Cross the center line and switch hand and leg again. Your inside hand asks the horse to look and bend into the direction he is traveling and the inside leg asks him to push his rib cage to the outside (away from leg pressure). Thus, the arc of his spine will match the arc of the half circle. Your goal is to make consistently round half circles and to cross the center line exactly halfway between each cone. Don't punish your horse if at first he is too close or too far away from the cones. He has to learn how close he should be to the cone. Remember, you are the driver—not the passenger. You must tell the horse where to go. Help him to meet the correct point between each set of cones to make the next half-circle. If you find that you are not meeting those exact center lines, make that your goal to work toward. Try to use more or less leg or more or less rein. In other words, adjust your cues until you find what your horse responds to the best.

The rein should feel soft in your hand as you ask him to bend. You should not feel as if you are pulling

4. She lightly gives to the bit and correctly follows the bend.

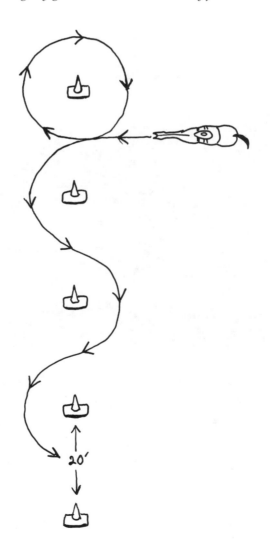

Here I over-cued and got too much bend. Rider error!

Counter-bending. This horse is arched slightly to the left, but moving diagonally forward to the right.

your horse around the entire half circle or feel him pulling on the bit. You should feel his rib cage move away from leg pressure at the girth. It will be most noticeable when you switch aids at the center point, for example when changing from left rein and left leg to right rein and right leg. You should feel the arc of the horse's body change under your seat.

TEACHING THE COUNTER-BEND

Work with your horse until he will make consistently round half circles between the cones. After both you and your horse master that exercise, begin to teach the horse to counter-bend or to move diagonally forward with a slight counter-bend in his body. The time spent bending your horse around your inside leg as you traveled through the serpentine pattern has given your horse some understanding that he must move away from leg pressure. If you don't feel the change in his body when you cross from one set of aids to the other (left leg and rein to circle left and right leg and rein to circle right), continue working on half or even full circles applying the same principles, before you advance to counter-bending. Do not jog the pattern staying straight close to the cones. You get the maximum benefit by making half circles between cones. Your horse should also willingly (softly) give you his face or flex at the poll in response to one-sided rein pressure.

To ask for the counter-bend maneuver, start with your horse parallel to a cone on your left. Walk straight forward a few feet past the cone to create forward motion. Now lift your right rein to create a slight bend in the horse's neck so that you can see just the corner of his right eye. Be sure to lift your hand straight above his mane to create the bend and let the rein merely touch his neck, suggesting a neck rein cue. Use only enough pressure to barely see the corner of his right eye. Too much rein pressure will cause too much bend. It will make the horse think that you are applying a direct rein cue. He will think that he should follow the direction of the rein cue. Your rein only creates the bend in the counter-bend maneuver. Your leg pushes the horse to the side and forward. His body should now be in a slight arc to the right. You must remember that this exercise uses more leg than rein. As you lift your right rein, immediately apply a strong right leg at the girth. Your right leg pressure cue applied at the girth will push your horse diagonally forward to the left. You should feel the horse cross over and step to the left.

Begin walking forward, parallel to the first cone for two to three steps, and then counter-bend to the left, using the right rein and right leg to push the horse over. The counter-bend maneuver will cause your horse to cross the long line of cones between two cones in a diagonal manner. For example, if you started on the left side of the cones, you will counter-bend for three to four steps to the left so you will then be on the right side of the cones. Release your cues to counter-bend and let the horse walk straight forward a few steps until you pass the second cone. Now apply the opposite aids—left rein and left leg to counter-bend right. Counter-bend until you cross the line of cones. Now you should be on the right side of the cones again. Walk straight ahead to pass the next cone and counter-bend in the opposite direction. Continue in this manner until you finish the line of cones.

If your horse begins to lead the counter-bend maneuver with his shoulder, you need to apply a slightly stronger rein aid to slow his shoulders and let his hind end catch up. If he leads with his hip, try a little less leg. You must find the correct balance of aids until your horse understands what you are asking. The goal is for the horse to stay parallel to the cones as he walks straight forward, and remain parallel to the cones while he counter-bends, although his body will be arced in whichever direction you asked him to bend. He will probably move in one direction better than the other, so be sure to work on both left and right sides until he can master either direction with ease. Soon you will be able to maneuver through the line of cones, counter-bending both left and right down the entire length of your arena.

Do not ask your horse to counter-bend continually without a break. Ask him to walk, jog, or lope around the arena, or work on other maneuvers, before asking again. Counter-bending is hard work for a horse. It stretches and supples his body in a way that he is unaccustomed. Your horse can get sore muscles just as you get sore by spending too much time in a gym or lifting too many hay bales. Do not over-do it and cause your horse to get sore and thus resentful.

PRACTICE FOR PERFECTION

Teaching a horse to follow the serpentine pattern between cones and later to counter-bend is the basis for all future lessons. When your horse has learned to move away from leg pressure, then you can ask him to sidepass. Contain his forward motion through the use of your reins and apply a leg cue to tell him he must move. The only option available is to sidepass to the left or right, depending upon which leg you used to cue him. In addition to teaching a horse to move away from leg pressure, these exercises teach your horse to give to one-sided rein pressure and to circle in a round or half-round circle—all things a trail horse must do with ease. You will be able to use your leg to push him out to the rail or to enlarge a circle or make it smaller, because he has learned that leg pressure means more than just "go."

Although this seems a simple maneuver to require weeks of practice, it is the basis for everything else you do in training your horse for trail. Although you can progress to other work as you continue to work on this pattern, do not skip over it.

Start slowly and gradually ask for more. In time, as you maneuver your horse through the cones bending and counter-bending, your horse should become more supple throughout his entire body and more responsive to your rein and leg aids. What once felt like a tug-of-war or a battle of wills will now take only a whisper of leg or rein pressure. Your horse's mind will become more in tune with your cues, and his supple, elastic body will allow him to perform these maneuvers with ease.

Arabian Horse and rider at a trail class. Photo © Mike Ferrara.

FOUR

LEG AND COLLECTION
THE HIDDEN CUES

THIS EXERCISE WILL BUILD on what you taught the horse by circling and serpentining through cones in the previous chapter. It will teach your horse to be maneuverable, flexible, and supple. You will ask the horse to circle in smaller and smaller diameters, using your legs to drive your horse forward into the bit and to push his hind legs up under him. Your horse will learn that no matter how small the circle you ask him to travel, he must continue at the same gait he started until he is cued differently.

This exercise will benefit you when a course requires that you make tight and demanding circles or corners over and through obstacles. Your horse will learn not to break gait when you apply your legs and squeeze him through a tight corner, telling him to maintain his impulsion. Once he understands the concepts gained through this exercise, he will no longer rush off when he feels your legs on his sides. He will accept collection more readily and will learn to use his entire body rather than just follow his nose.

Teaching your horse to be supple throughout his entire body will make him more flexible, and could save him from discomfort or injury. An uncomfortable horse will become resentful, which will show in his attitude. As

trail classes become more and more competitive, you want everything in your favor. A horse with a good attitude is one more plus.

BEGIN THE CIRCLING EXERCISE

You do not need an arena. You can do this exercise in an open field or any flat area. However, if you do work in an arena, the easiest way to do this exercise is to come off the path on the edge of your arena and go directly into this circling exercise. Start with five cones. Put the first cone on the inside edge of the path of your arena or field so that you can leave the path and go directly into the circling maneuver. Put another cone ten feet away from the first cone to the inside. This second cone is your center point. Add a third cone ten feet past the second cone. These three cones are in a line. The fourth cone is ten feet towards the top of the arena and the fifth, ten feet to the bottom, creating a visible circle around the center cone.

The second or middle cone is the one you will circle around. The other cones are markers to keep you in the correct size of circle. Begin with the cones set ten feet from the center cone, and over the period of a month or two

1. *Come off the rail to circle the middle cone (not visible in this photo), staying inside the outside guide cones. The first cone is behind the horse's right back leg.*

2. *Drive with your legs to maintain the jog as you circle the middle cone, staying inside the top and bottom cone.*

3. *Continue around the cone, driving with your legs if needed. . .*

4. *. . .until you complete the circle and exit.*

adjust them so they are eight feet from the center. That is the tightest circle you will need.

This exercise can also be done without cones, but using the cones will help you to learn the size of the circle that you must make for this exercise to be beneficial and effective. After you have memorized the size of the circle, discontinue using the cones for markers and practice in any flat area.

Begin at a walk. Ask your horse to walk forward with impulsion. As you come to the set of cones, take your inside rein (the rein next to the cones)

and ask your horse to make a small circle around the middle cone. Try to stay within the outside marker cones. Your goal is to make a round circle—not oblong, not oval, and not egg-shaped. Your horse may begin this exercise by making different shaped "circles." Your goal is to teach him that you want round circles. Ask your horse to use himself and bend around the circles. His head and neck might be over-bent for this exercise, which will help to supple his neck and enforce obedience. His spine should bend around the cone as he turns.

To ask him to circle, first gain light contact with the bit with your inside (directional) rein. Hold your hand at the top of your hip. You should just barely feel the horse's mouth. The other rein must be loose to allow the horse to bend his head to such a degree. Now lift your left hand up even higher to ask the horse to circle, perhaps ten to twelve inches higher than you started, until the horse's head is almost at a forty-five degree angle and you can see the entire side of his face. He should be looking into the circle. Keep your rein up to be sure that he does not drop his shoulder into the circle, negating the benefit of this exercise. Use your legs and squeeze the horse to drive him around the circle. Squeezing your legs drives his rear under him and it will give him the impulsion to move around the entire circle without breaking gait. The smallness of the circle keeps him from charging forward. When you have completed the circle, release all pressure and let your horse walk forward out of the circle.

If at any time your horse tries to reach down and take the rein out of your hand, make him circle. Use this same method as a correction. This will lift his head and put his attention back on you without jerking on his mouth. Small circles are uncomfortable for a horse and he will want to avoid the behavior that caused him to be corrected by a tight circle.

ADVANCE TO THE JOG

Repeat the circling exercise until you are comfortable with the maneuver, then advance to a jog. The above distances are set for a jog so you will not have to change the distance of the cones. First, jog around the arena until your horse is settled and jogging with

Keep your hand up as you circle to keep the horse's shoulder up.

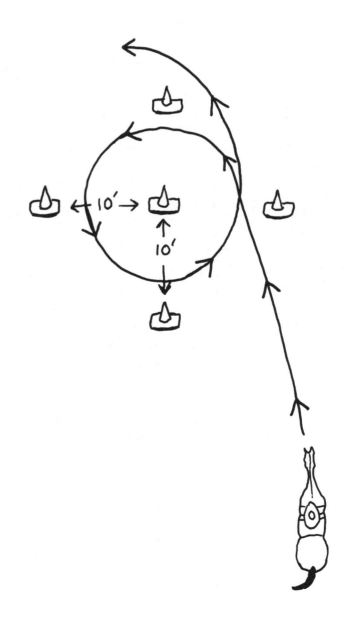

some impulsion, not speed. (If you go into the circle with your horse barely moving his feet, he will fizzle out and break to a walk before you barely begin to circle.) When you get to the cones, lift your inside rein hand to ask the horse to circle around the center cone staying within the markers, and squeeze with your legs. If you execute this correctly, you will see the entire side of the horse's head with almost a forty-five degree bend in his neck. Don't worry if you don't get it the first time or two. Just continue to practice and it will come in time. Squeeze your legs to drive the horse into the bridle and around the turn. The smallness of the circle will keep him from running and teach him to accept this much leg pressure, which will help you later. He is learning that leg pressure and the opposing rein means to lift his back and collect rather than to speed up and move faster. Increase the amount of leg pressure if the horse breaks back to a walk. You must use a continuous, strong squeeze (not a kick) all the way around the circle.

Watched from the ground, the horse's front legs will cross one another as he makes the turn. You will notice this more as you tighten the circle. Drive him forward with your legs at a jog around the entire circle. Release the pressure and let him go back to the rail when you finish the circle. Remember that this is hard work, especially for a horse that is not fit and supple. As his body suppleness improves, so will his ability to circle tightly and correctly, driving off his hind end and bending his head and neck.

If the horse tries to fade to the outside of the circle, lift your inside rein hand higher, straight above his mane to lift his shoulder and cause him to stay upright and balanced between the bridle. If your horse tries to drop his inside shoulder into the circle, then move your rein hand an inch or two across his mane, keeping your hand up. A horse cannot drop his shoulder if he is bent correctly. Bringing your hand slightly across his neck as you lift and turn will force him to bend. Drive him on with your legs. Play with varying amounts of pressure until your horse will circle around the center cone in a round circle without bumping the outside cones. Many horses won't get it right the first time or even the first week or two. Keep schooling, incorporating five to ten minutes of circling work throughout your daily training routine.

Incorporate this exercise into your daily schooling routine. One day your horse will suddenly understand and you'll feel the thrill of knowing that your schooling is beginning to pay off. Training takes time. All horses go through spells where it seems they never grasp the concept and, suddenly, one day they do. That one day is well-worth the time spent. Depending upon the age of your horse and his ability, your ability, and the amount of time that you ride and school, this may take a month or more. Your horse will benefit from whatever time you school on this exercise, so don't give up or stop.

MAKE THE CIRCLES TIGHTER

When your horse can stay inside the cones placed ten feet apart, then move them to nine feet apart. Repeat until the horse can handle this distance with ease. Then change the cones to eight feet from center to center. This is the maximum tightness that you will need to benefit from this exercise. A smaller horse may be able to circle even tighter, while a very large horse might find this distance tight. Setting the cones at eight feet should allow you to gain the maximum benefit from this exercise for most horses.

Your goal is a perfectly round circle with the horse crossing the outside front leg over the inside front leg, as he turns and drives his hind legs up under himself. Strive to keep an even cadence to the jog.

After you have maneuvered through these cones for a while, you should be able to feel what size circle is correct. At that point, you can circle at any point in your arena and do away with the cones completely. Without the cones, your horse will have to depend on your cues, rather than on the cones. Beginning with the cones, or incorporating the cones in your schooling at some point in time, will give your horse the chance to adjust to maneuvering around cones. Cones are included in many trail classes as markers. Since you introduced your horse to the cones in a tight setting such as this, he should barely give them a glance when faced with cones at a show.

LOPE THE CIRCLES

Once your horse feels as if he understands the concept of moving in a tight circle at a jog, you may ask him to lope a circle, using the same type of pattern, but a larger circle. You will not have nearly the degree of bend in your horse's neck as you did at the jog. Just ask for his neck and spine to be bent in the same arc as the circle itself. Be sure to lift your reins up. Lope around the edge of your arena or work area and guide your horse into a medium

EQUIPMENT

As you begin this exercise, outfit your horse in a snaffle bit and a running martingale. Adjust the rings so that they are on the same line that a rein running from the bit to the saddle horn would be. If your horse lugs on the bit or is unresponsive in a snaffle, experiment with a somewhat thinner mouthpiece. I begin this exercise within the first few months of starting a colt, while he is still in a snaffle. I prefer a snaffle to begin with because I use contact on the bit to make the horse give me his head and circle tightly. A snaffle uses a direct pull, so the signals coming from the bit are easy for the horse to understand. The running martingale keeps the horse from raising his head in the air to avoid bit pressure and helps to keep his head in the correct position during the initial stages of training. When the horse understands and will perform this exercise with ease, you can switch to your customary bit. Continue to use a running martingale until your horse consistently drops his head into the bit and no longer tries to fight the rein signal by raising his head.

If your horse is unresponsive in a snaffle, use your customary bit, but remember that when circling you are adding leverage from the shanks that can cause conflicting signals. Be sure to lift up on the rein rather than out. Lifting up has the additional benefit of asking your horse to flex at the poll as he turns.

Teaching your horse to maintain a consistent pace will help with jog-overs and lope-overs.

the smallness of the circle teach the horse to slow his lope. A small circle naturally forces him to slow. If he races around a small circle, he will fall on his face and he knows it. Use the circle to your benefit. Once your horse is comfortable with this exercise at the lope, then you can begin to ask for more collection by squeezing him up into the bridle a little more with your legs and tightening the circle.

Many trail course patterns include jog-overs and lope-overs, so your horse will need to learn to move with collection so that he can master these obstacles. A horse that jogs or lopes all strung out will stumble through a jog- or lope-over obstacle. A horse needs to use himself correctly to master these new and tougher obstacles. Jog-overs and lope-overs will be discussed more in a later chapter. This chapter is devoted to teaching your horse to master circles and teaching you to use your hands and legs.

FRAME UP

Because you have taught your horse the basics of circling correctly and giving to the bit as you apply your leg aids, you can use a circle to put your horse back in the correct frame. Framing up in a circle should be comfortable to the horse now. When a trail horse is in the correct "frame," he is softly flexed at the pole. His face is vertical, or slightly in front of vertical. His back will be rounded and will rise under your seat because he is driving off his hindquarters, lifting his middle and using his body correctly. A horse's "engine" is located in his hindquarters. He should push himself forward with his rear legs , not pull himself forward with his forelegs.

You must teach your horse to use his body to his maximum potential,

sized circle at a lope. When you complete the circle, let him go back to the rail still at a lope. Once he will lope a medium-size circle, ask him to make it smaller. Begin to use your legs lightly to squeeze him up into the bridle, although not as strongly as you did at the jog—unless your horse is naturally lazy. If he tries to break back to a jog, use more leg pressure. If he tries to move too fast, release a little leg pressure and make your circle a little smaller. Try to use your reins only to guide the horse into a circle rather than to pull him back to slow him. Let

much like a highly trained gymnast. Remember, the horse does not "frame up" because you pull on his face to make him flex at the poll. Instead, the forward energy is generated in his hindquarters as a result of you using your legs to drive him forward into the bit. You "capture" that forward energy by the use of your reins.

If you look at a horse that is traveling out of frame, his back is hollow and he may appear strung out because he is taking long, reaching strides with his front legs. His spine will dip slightly under the rider's seat. A horse that is traveling in frame, on the other hand, will take small, collected steps.

Traveling in frame is something that you must ask your horse to do over and over until he knows exactly what is expected of him. When riding two-handed in a snaffle, if your horse loses his frame as he travels around the arena, you can use the corners to "fix" your horse. A corner is really just a quarter of a circle. Use it to remind your horse of the proper position. Apply a little more pressure on your inside rein and squeeze your legs. This tells the horse to take the corner (which he would do anyway in an arena without barely a cue from you); yet to a judge it only looks as if you are cueing your horse to bend around the corner. If you squeeze your legs and use slight extra pressure on that inside rein in a similar manner as you did when practicing the circles, your horse should reach down into the bit, flex at the poll and adjust his cadence. Performing circles correctly into the bit and maintaining the correct cadence should be a familiar and an established routine to your horse. If you ever find that you must move off the rail in a rail class to make a circle to put yourself in a better position, you will look forward to circles rather than dreading moving off the rail. Circles give you the chance to put your horse back in frame. In a trail class, your entire ride is off the rail, so use those corners, circles, or half-circles to your benefit—as a wake up call to your horse; or to readjust and maintain his cadence, impulsion, collection and frame.

Don't look down or look at the pole. You'll cause your horse to step where you look.

1. *If your horse travels strung out like this (notice the long steps with nose pointing out). . .*

2. *. . .lift both reins and squeeze with your legs to drive the horse up into the bridle.*

3. *Then release. Compare the the length of the horse's steps to the first photo.*

4. *Here, the mare has shortened her steps and lifted her back, i.e., collection, but she needs a reminder to flex at the poll.*

FLEX, SQUEEZE, LIFT AND COLLECT

Once your horse understands to drop his head and flex into the bit on first one side and then on the other from the circling exercises, begin to ask the horse to flex at the poll in a straight line. Take even contact with both reins and gradually tighten the reins as you squeeze the horse up into the bit (with your legs) until the horse is really into the bridle or deeply flexed at the poll. Hold the reins steady at the point where you want the horse flexed. Do not continue to pull. Never ask a horse to flex so deeply that his nose is tucked into his chest. If a horse learns to do that, he has an easy way to evade all reins cues, including the one that means to stop. Gradually take the horse's nose back towards his chest until his face is vertical with the ground or possibly an inch past vertical. At that point, hold your reins steady and squeeze your legs so that your horse continues to move forward. If he tries to stop, you must use more leg pressure. If he cannot grasp what you are asking of him, you may have to use less rein pressure and allow his head to be a little ahead of the vertical for a few days until he does understand what you want. You may have to squeeze quite hard initially. Be sure that you have done the prior exercises, otherwise simply pulling on a horse's mouth could cause him to rear. If you use rein pressure without the accompanying leg pressure, the horse will stop from the "pull." You must use your legs to push him into the bit.

I find it best to begin this exercise at a jog. Hold this extremely collected position for ten strides and then let your reins slide from your hands as you stop squeezing with your legs. Remember, collection is caused by leg pressure urging a horse on, with the reins slowing his forward motion. Because he cannot reach forward and "go," the horse must reach further underneath himself, moving up and down and thus achieving collection.

I often do this exercise with the horse in a snaffle bit so that I can take hold of his mouth without fear of hurting him. You can use this exercise with a shank bit, but take care not to apply too much rein pressure, which could cause a horse to rear or even flip over. Use just enough pressure that the horse flexes at the poll and use your legs to drive him forward. Remember—never pull—just hold and drive with your legs.

When your horse is comfortable with the above exercise, and has advanced to a shank bit, ask your horse to jog. Take both reins halfway up the horse's neck and lift them straight up towards the sky—just enough to cause the horse to flex at the poll with his face vertical with the ground—as you squeeze the horse up into the bridle. This has the effect of

This horse is carrying his head a little too high.

A lift and release reminds him where it should be carried.

causing the horse to lift and round his back as he flexes at the poll. This exercise helps a horse to jog correctly in a two-beat gait: one, two, one, two, one, two. You will feel his back lift up and hit you in the seat. His steps will shorten as he reaches upwards with his legs rather than forward, the result of collection. Ask him to maintain this collected position for fifty feet and then gradually let the reins slide forward through your fingers. Wait a minute or two as you jog around and then repeat. As he learns to hold this position, gradually ask him to hold it longer. Work on this for five to ten minutes every day and you will see your horse's jog improve. It will teach him to use his rear end, rather than let it drag behind him, and it will force him to jog correctly in a true two-beat gait rather than jog in front and walk behind.

When your horse is comfortable with this exercise at a jog, start over with the same steps and ask him to lope. Ask him to flex and collect for five strides and then add a few more strides as he understands. Incorporate periods of this exercise at both the jog and lope for a few minutes every day and you should see an improvement in your horse's gaits and responsiveness.

As a result of the above exercises, after you advance to riding one-handed, a couple of light bumps upward on the reins as you lightly squeeze your legs will cause your horse to drop his head and flex at the poll. He should also round his back and readjust his cadence. When riding one-handed, this gives you the same benefit that riding circles does when riding two-handed. Riding one-hand-

Even a finished horse needs correction from time to time to keep him framed up and on the bit. Here I have over-flexed briefly as a reminder to obey. Do not let the horse travel this way all the time.

ed, you can lightly lift and bump your reins upwards and squeeze your legs as a reminder to the horse to drop his head to the correct position and maintain his gait in a cadenced rhythm. After many months of schooling, your goal is to have your horse maintain his head position, collection, and cadence without any reminders from you, whether he is moving from one obstacle to the next, going through an obstacle, or traveling on the rail.

WORK TOWARD THE GOAL

Your goal for this exercise, and one that is most helpful to your future trail horse, is to be able to jog, and later lope, a tight turn almost in place. When you are asked to make a tight turn from one obstacle to the next, you can squeeze your legs and push the horse forward with the correct impulsion. If he begins to speed up, a light lift of the reins should be all that it takes to correct him. Your horse will learn to maintain his jog, and eventually his lope, as he turns, almost in place. He will learn to use his body and be responsive to your cues. He will no longer surge forward when he feels your legs closing in on him, and he will not fizzle out on a tight corner and break gait. He readily understands the cue to keep him moving and will flex at the poll in response to a light rein cue and reach underneath himself to collect when he feels your legs. This prevents him from stumbling through obstacles or dragging his feet on the ground. Your confidence in his ability will allow you to sit up and look ahead, allowing your horse to maneuver over or through demanding obstacles without a change in your weight affecting his balance. You should be able to sit still, trust your horse, and let him do his job.

FIVE

THE HORSESHOE PATTERN

INCORPORATING this simple exercise into your daily schooling routine will help your horse learn to wait for and obey your cues. If your horse will move away from leg pressure and understands the concept of neck reining, he should be able to perform this simple pattern with relative ease. As you continue to school, this maneuver will help his lope departures by setting him up correctly to depart into the correct lead from almost a standstill. It will help his lope, lope to halt transitions, and turn on the haunches (or 180 degree turn in place). It also forces you to become a rider, rather than a passenger.

A large part of the success of this exercise is that you are constantly "changing your horse's mind." He cannot depend on the rail or fence and just go round and round the arena. Used correctly, the horseshoe maneuver will teach your horse that he must wait for, and obey, your cues. It will cure him of anticipating, teach him to depart into a lope, make a lope to halt transition, and turn in place, planting his hind pivot foot.

RIDING THE PATTERN

When he is warmed up and ready to work, take your horse off the rail and lope up the long side of your arena, fifteen to twenty feet inside the rail. Your actual distance from the rail does not matter as long as your horse cannot depend on the fence. He should look to you for direction.

As you reach the top of your arena, make a half-circle, following the fence line, yet still keeping the same distance away from the fence. Continue down the other long side of the arena. At the bottom of the second long side you will make what looks like a horseshoe, hence the name for this exercise. At this point, ask your horse to halt. Don't be overly concerned if your horse does not stop perfectly. This exercise, used over a period of time, will help.

To ask for a stop, pick up both reins to elevate his shoulders and put his weight back over his hocks. Next, use your leg on the inside of the horse shoe to ask the horse to move away from leg pressure and to turn in place towards the outside of the arena.

Pick up your reins and elevate the horse's shoulders so he cannot walk forward out of the turn. Elevating his shoulders puts his weight back over his hocks. He will learn to plant his hind pivot foot and cross over with his front legs because his weight is back over his hocks, in response to

1. Lope up the long side of the arena, 15 to 20 feet inside the rail, and stop. Lift your reins to shift the horse's weight to the rear.

2. Begin the turn by cueing with a right neck rein and left leg cue to tell the horse to pivot to the right.

3. She should pivot around her right hind foot.

4. She may slightly readjust her pivot foot, although it stays basically in position.

your leg cue. Your goal, the end result, is to have him plant his pivot foot and make the turn crossing over (not behind) with his front legs as he turns the half circle in place. That sets him up to depart into a lope.

When the horse has completed the 180-degree turn in place and is facing the opposite direction, apply your outside leg at the girth to ask him to immediately depart into a lope up the long side of the arena once again. (If you normally use a different cue for a lope departure, then use that cue now.) Ask for the lope as soon as the horse has made the turn. His next step will be with his outside rear leg, which sets him up perfectly for an inside lead lope. Because of the way his weight is positioned, he is set up to push off correctly and depart into a lope almost from a standstill. Again, don't worry if you do not get a perfect response in the initial stages. This exercise will teach the horse to use his hind end and depart correctly. Keep asking, and after a period of time you will see his response improve.

A SAMPLE RUN

Begin your lope on the left-hand side of the arena with the fence on your left. Follow the horseshoe pattern, stopping with the fence on your left at the bottom of the other side of the arena. Elevate your horse's shoulders and apply a light, right neck rein cue. Simultaneously, use your inside leg (right leg in this example) to ask the horse to make a 180-degree turn in place towards the fence. After he completes the turn, the fence should be on your right. Now your right leg is your outside leg. Cue for the for the left or inside lead lope with your right leg. Lope the horseshoe pattern again. Make the half circle at the top of the

The horse's next step after the pivot is with the left hind foot, which naturally sets her up for an inside, right lead. As she completes the turn, cue for lope (right lead in this example). For a right lead lope, she departs on the left hind. This is followed by her right hind and left front leg, and finally by the leading, or inside (right) foreleg.

Lope the horseshoe until you reach the other side. Then reverse the cues and repeat. Notice this mare's soft, slow, collected lope.

arena as before and then lope down the long side before asking him to stop at the bottom of the "horseshoe." The fence is still on your right. This time, use your left (inside) leg to ask the horse to do a 180-degree turn in place to the right, and cue with your left leg to ask the horse to depart immediately into the lope. His next step, after pivoting on his right hind leg to make the turn, is to step with his left hind leg. This sets him up correctly for a right-lead lope. Repeat the exercise.

THE BENEFITS

This exercise has many benefits, however, if you continue to ride this pattern exactly as stated, over and over, your horse will begin to anticipate the lope, halt, turn, and lope-off. To be sure that doesn't happen, change the pattern from time to time. Rather than stopping at the bottom of the horse shoe, continue to lope around the inside of the arena (the same distance away from the fence) for two or three circles before repeating the horse shoe pattern.

Another variation is to stop at the top of the arena and ride what looks like an upside-down horseshoe. Or, make two or three circles that are half the size of your arena. You could also make your stop half way down the long side of the arena. As your horse becomes proficient at this exercise, lope across the short side of your arena, halt, turn and lope again. You can ride the horseshoe pattern upside down, right side up, or sideways to the left or right. The key is to keep the horse guessing what you will ask for next. Don't let him anticipate. Make him wait for your cues.

Asking for a halt, lope, and halt will cause your horse to slow his lope, anticipating the halt. Because you set him up correctly to take the inside lead, it is easy for him to learn the cue for each lead and to depart into the lope from a standstill. (Be sure to ask for each lead consistently, using the same cue every time.) He learns to push off into the lope correctly. Loping the small half-circle at the top of the horseshoe teaches your horse to collect and use his body. Lifting your reins to make the 180-degree turn in place, helps him to elevate his shoulders and plant his inside hind pivot foot. You gain control over his entire body.

This is a simple exercise to incorporate into your daily lessons. It teaches your horse to wait for, to respect, and to obey your cues. This type of control is necessary if you plan to teach your horse to maneuver in tight trail courses. Your horse must obey your every cue. The time spent now will pay dividends down the trail. Although many people think the obstacles are the only focus of a trail class, that is simply not true. You need to be in complete control of every step that your horse makes, and his gaits between obstacles are an important part of the picture.

As soon as your horse masters this maneuver and you have read the chapter on the lope-overs and practiced riding over poles, you can incorporate loping over poles into the horseshoe patterns. Start with a single lope-over pole on the straight line, and add poles as your horse masters going over the single pole in stride. Eventually you can place the poles on the curved top of the horseshoe. But, remember, take each maneuver step by step and add a degree of difficulty only after your horse understands the simple, beginning steps of each maneuver.

SIX

CIRCLES

AFTER YOUR HORSE learns to move in a frame, flexed at the poll with his body collected and his power coming from his hindquarters as discussed in the previous chapters, you can begin to work on the small circles and turns that are sometimes required in a trail course. Because we are talking about trail horses that are required to get off the rail and perform in the center of the arena, it only makes sense to get off the rail and lope some circles in the center of the arena. Lope both large and small circles. Circle to

While training, keep your inside rein up as you cue for a circle to prevent the horse from dropping a shoulder.

Whether walking, jogging, or loping—always keep the inside rein up when circling.

the left and to the right. Circle at a jog or trot, too, working both sides of the horse's body.

If you feel the horse "falling into the circle" (dropping his inside shoulder and leaning to the inside like a motorcycle cornering), take your inside rein and lift it straight up. This will lift his shoulder and get him traveling upright and balanced once again. Lift him up, balance him, release and go on. Repeat the same sequence of cues every time that he drops his shoulder. He must stay upright and balanced.

If you are circling and the horse swings or throws his hip to the outside of your circle, use your outside leg behind the girth to push his hip back into the correct arc of the circle. If you are unsure, ask a ground person to tell you when your horse is not arcing his body or correctly maintaining the same arc as the circle. If a light leg cue behind the girth does not hold your horse's outside hip in the correct arc of the circle, bump with your heel and continue to bump until you feel his hip move back in line. Use spurs if he ignores your heel. Keep your horse's temperament in mind if you choose this corrective measure. Some horses will hardly move with a thump from your heel, while others will be off and running at the lightest touch. Fit your cues to the horse. By now you should have a good feel for the amount of correction your horse requires.

Begin the circle exercise at a jog, and when your horse has mastered the basics of circling correctly and maintaining his gait at a jog, then ask him to lope. Start with larger circles and gradually, over a period of weeks, begin to make them smaller. An easy way to start riding round circles is to mark out the four "corners" of a circle and then ride a rounded line from cone to cone. Milk jugs filled with sand or any other type of marker can be substituted for cones. The idea is to become familiar with what a round circle rides and feels like so that you can help your horse to follow a round path and to stay upright and balanced. Later, when you add jog- or lope-over obstacles that are on a curved line, you will be able to feel if your horse is correct, and either leave him alone or correct him as needed. The more correct you ask your horse to be, the sooner he will understand what is acceptable and what is not acceptable.

Teaching a horse to follow his nose and arc correctly around a circle takes work. You must know what is correct and what is wrong so you can correct it. And, you must practice until riding a correct circle is automatic for both you and your horse.

I use circling to teach a horse that he must be obedient. Riding along the rail or fence line only teaches a horse to follow the rail. When you leave the rail and ride in the wide open spaces or in the center of the arena, the horse must pay attention to you. He must be prepared for you to ask for changes of direction, changes of gaits, and, in general, learn to do what you ask, when you ask him to do it.

Your horse may resist the bend at first.

Over a period of days, you will notice his response improving.

COUNTER CANTERING

Some trail courses require that you counter canter all or part of a circle. A horse that changes leads automatically will cause you to lose points. Therefore, you must teach your trail horse that you, not he, chooses the time to change leads. A good exercise is to lope three or four circles half the size of your arena in one direction. Then, without breaking gait, ask your horse to counter canter—use the same lead but circle in the opposite direction. Do that by keeping the leg that you use to cue for the lead on your horse's side as you keep his shoulders up. Keeping your leg on his side tells him that you want him to be on the counter lead. Without changing leads, change directions again and lope in your original direction a few times. Teach the horse that changing directions does not automatically mean

that he must (or can) change leads. Counter cantering a circle is strenuous for a horse and not something that you want to drill on. But, if your horse continues to switch leads even when he is not asked, counter cantering will teach him to watch for and obey your cues. If he switches unasked, put him right back on the opposite lead and make him stay in the counter canter until you ask for a change of direction that puts him back on the correct lead. As with every exercise, start easily and gradually increase the degree of difficulty.

POA trail pony class photograph. Photo © Paula J. Nulik.

SEVEN

THE BACK-UP

A BACKING OBSTACLE is mandatory, at least in the American Quarter Horse Association rules, with minimum distances between markers to keep the obstacles uniform. The minimum space between the poles, logs or markers that you are required to back between is twenty-eight to thirty-six inches, depending on the type of obstacle. The minimum changes to thirty inches if the back-up poles are elevated. The elevation of the poles may be no higher than twenty-four inches.

BACK-THROUGH OBSTACLES

The back-up obstacle may be set up in many ways. You might be required to back straight or through an "L," a "V," or "U" shape. You could also be required to back through and around at least three markers, usually cones. You may find three cones set in a triangle, which requires that you back through the first two cones, around the second cone, and then back through the first two cones. Your backing steps, if drawn on paper, would look similar to the bottom of a light bulb. On occasion, two logs, placed at right angles to each other, outline the base of the obstacle to be

sure that you don't back too far out as you maneuver around the second cone. Another type of backing obstacles has three markers set in a straight line and which you must serpentine through backwards. These can also be outlined with poles. The "L," "V," and "U" shaped obstacles are self explanatory, although illustrations are included.

THE FIRST STEP BACK

Before you can consider backing through any of the above obstacles, you must first teach your horse to take one step backwards. If you taught your horse to flex at the poll in response to rein pressure, teaching the reverse usually is not all that difficult. It may take a few minutes for the horse to understand that not only must he flex at the poll in response to rein pressure, he must also back.

One of the hidden benefits of teaching a horse to back is that it helps a horse to understand to flex at the poll in response to rein pressure. Be sure that he doesn't pull the reins through your hands when you ask him to back up and therefore reward himself by getting a release. Insist that your horse gives you his head, and

Ask your horse to back one step.

Reward him by releasing the reins.

then encourage him to take a step back. (Unless, of course, he becomes fractious and tries to rear or some other dangerous maneuver.)

To ask for the back-up, first walk your horse forward and then ask him to stop. It confuses a horse in the initial stages of training if you grab his mouth from a standstill and ask him to back. Put the odds in your favor. After he stops, be sure to reward him for stopping by releasing your rein pressure. Then pick up both reins evenly and slowly take the slack out of the reins until you gain contact with

the horse's mouth. Eventually, your horse will begin to flex at the poll and back before you actually gain contact with his mouth. He will feel the reins lifting up his neck and respond to that cue if you keep your rein signal soft. If you snatch at the reins and jerk upward on his mouth, the first thing a horse will do is to throw his head in the air. The grab and snatch will scare him. Combined with the pain of the jerk on his mouth, it will send his head upwards (when the proper response is to drop, flex at the poll, and back softly). Take the slack out of the reins slowly and continue with a slow upward movement of your hand until you have contact with the horse's mouth. Continue moving your hands upward until your horse flexes at the poll and takes a step back. Do not release that pressure until he takes at least one step backward

In the initial stages of training, saying the word "Back" is acceptable. The horse should understand the word back from being backed on the ground, and speaking the word initially will help him to understand what you want. In addition to the rein cue, squeeze your legs on his sides and cluck. The leg pressure and cluck tells him that he must move, yet the rein pressure blocks forward motion. The only place left for the horse to go is backwards. When he takes one step back, immediately release all pressure. Praise the horse verbally or scratch his neck the first few times. When he understands the cues, omit the praise or he will come to expect it every time. Let your horse rest a moment to think about what he did that caused him to be rewarded. Then ask again, using the exact same sequence of cues. Get one step back and immediately release pressure. Let him rest briefly to absorb what he did and repeat it a third time. Then work on other maneuvers.

I use the "three-time rule" in the initial stages of asking a horse to back. Ask three times and then work on something else. Repeat the three sequences later in your lesson. Repeat it once more at the end of your lesson. Let it absorb into his brain over night. By the following day, your horse should respond more readily. Remember, what you teach a horse today, he learns tomorrow. Use that concept to your advantage. It will save both you and your horse much aggravation.

HOW TO APPLY THE CUE

You will need backwards directional control in a trail horse, for example to cue him to make a backwards turn in an "L" shape. Squeeze with your calves and save your heel pressure behind the girth to move the hip of the horse left or right—away from pressure—to tell him to turn while backing. Remember, the hip always leads in a back-up. Pick up your reins slowly to block the horse's forward movement and to signal the back. Apply your legs by squeezing your calves and cluck as the cue that he must "move somewhere." Because your reins block his forward movement, the only option left to the horse is to go backward.

Some people teach their horses to back up as they lift the rein and apply a light pull for each step backwards. Rather than hold the rein steady, they lift, release, lift, release. Either method is acceptable. Personally, I think the lift and hold method is just a little neater. You have less hand movement to draw attention to the fact that you are cueing the horse. To stop his backward motion, simply move your rein hand down closer to his mane to release the pressure. In either case, give just a light touch on the mouth. Do not pull the horse backwards with his mouth gap-

Lift the reins to cue the horse to back.

ing open in protest. If your horse does that, have his teeth checked and make certain there are no other problems in his mouth.

If his mouth checks out okay, go back to basics and teach him how to back. You will lose points if he shows resistance in his mouth when backing.

TROUBLE SHOOTING THE BACK-UP

If your horse does not grasp the concept of backing, you should dismount and ask him to back from the ground, using your reins to ask him to back. Recreate the same line of "pull" from the reins that your horse would feel if you were mounted—straight from his mouth to your hand. It is beneficial if you teach your horse to back on a lead line long before he is broke to saddle. Use a verbal command, "Back," if you've previously taught him to back on that command from the ground. Discontinue the verbal command after he understands to back solely from the rein cue. Tapping the horse on his chest will help him to understand that he is to back up, but remember that your goal is to get him to obey a rein signal while you are mounted.

Another cue to tell your horse to back while you are mounted is curling your hip bones slightly under and forward. Do not lean back and lose the straight line from your head to your shoulders and hips. Just slightly shift some of your weight, taking some of it off the saddle and putting it into your stirrups as you curl your hips slightly forward. Your horse is very capable of learning that these slight shifts in your body are additional cues. If you consistently use them, they can become your sole cues. But you must be sure you use them every time.

Once your horse begins to show his understanding of your back up cues, then you can ask for two steps, then three, then four, and so forth. The first time or two that your horse backs, be happy when he takes one good step backwards with his head flexed, his mouth quiet, and no resistance showing in his body. Once he masters that, ask for additional steps. In a week or two he should be backing correctly for four or five steps. However, if it takes longer, let him learn at his pace. There is no set timetable in training horses. You must proceed at his pace, not yours.

DIRECTING THE BACK-UP

If your horse tries to veer in either direction when backing, use your legs to guide or correct him. For example, if your horse tries to swing his hip to the left, use your left leg behind the girth to push his hind end to the right and back in line. If he tries to swing his hip to the right, use your right leg to push his hip back in line. Practice asking your horse to back in

a controlled, straight line. After he has mastered backing in a straight line, teach him to move his hip either left or right in response to your leg cues.

The horse's hip always leads in the back-up. To make a turn in reverse, you must first cue his hip to turn and then apply a rein signal to direct his front end. Make his front end follow his hind end, much like following a trailer backwards with your truck. Train your horse to back between three cones in a serpentine pattern. Set the cones—you can use three, six, or even eight cones to practice—six to twelve feet apart for training purposes. As your horse gains understanding of this maneuver, slowly tighten the distance to thirty-six or forty inches, which is what you will find at a show. As your horse becomes really polished at backing in a controlled manner, you can set the distances between the cones slightly closer. If your horse can back between cones placed thirty-four inches apart, when asked to back between cones set thirty-six inches apart at a show, it will be a piece of cake for him. He is used to maneuvering in tighter distances. However, never start off with the cones this close together or you will confuse the horse. Let him learn the obstacle first, and then slowly, over a period of time, shorten the distances. Always make it easy in the initial stages of training. Don't scare your horse by asking too much on his first attempts. Add a slight degree of difficulty as the horse learns each step and continue in this manner, adding step by step, until you achieve the finished maneuver.

THE SERPENTINE BACK-UP

Start by lining your horse up parallel to the left side of the first cone, with your foot beside the cone. Back straight backward for a couple of steps to get past the cone. To make the turn between cones, apply left leg pressure slightly behind the girth. (Pressure at the girth would tell the horse to side pass.) This pushes the horse's hip to the right and leads the way through the turn. Once his hip starts to swing correctly between the cones, apply a right neck rein (or left direct rein) to tip the horse's head to the left. Now you should be between the cones.

To turn your horse's hip to the left to serpentine around the middle cone, apply right leg pressure to push his hip to the left. As his hip starts to swing to the left, apply a left neck rein (or right direct rein) to make his front end follow his hip around the turn. As he passes the middle cone, apply left leg pressure to swing his hip to the right. Follow with the right neck rein (or left direct rein cue) to swing the horse's front end parallel to the left side of the cone. He should finish parallel to the third cone. If you have more cones in a line to serpentine in a backwards manner, continue, using the same method until you have finished the line of cones. I sometimes ask a horse to back the length of my arena, serpentining through six or seven cones, when training for a trail class. Backing builds the muscles in the rear, as well as teaching the horse to obey your cues to move both left and right in reverse.

THE L-SHAPED BACK-UP

Before you negotiate the L-shaped back-up, first practice the L-shaped corner without poles. Your horse must obey your cues to turn in reverse both with and without poles. Horses that have practiced the L-shaped back-though with the poles on the ground will go through with barely a cue.

First, however, you must back a few steps to get to the corner of the

"L." Those few steps allow your horse to think "back-up." Your hands control the horse's front and your legs control his hip. It is easiest if you picture a pole running down through your horse's withers, much like a merry-go-round pole. The horse will pivot ninety-degrees around the imaginary pole running through his center. Once he makes the turn, release your hand and leg cues and then use your straight back cues to finish the "L." Let your horse stand for a moment to absorb what he did. If you rush right off to perform the same or a different maneuver, he might interpret that as a correction. Instead, let him stand for a minute or two. The brief rest tells him he performed correctly and is being rewarded. It also keeps him from rushing in a class. He will learn to stand patiently and wait for your cue to tell him what to do next.

When you have mastered the turn in reverse, put poles on the ground and back through those. First, walk your horse forward through the poles and ask him to back out. This teaches him that logs or poles are nothing to fear. Learning that he can maneuver between the poles while walking forward builds confidence that he can maneuver through them in reverse. Then, ask him to back through the "L" two or three times and go on to another exercise (provided, of course, that your horse is not fighting you or had a really bad trip through the poles). Always end a lesson on the best possible note. Look for a slight understanding or improvement. Come back to the exercise later if you want to practice it again. Your horse will become frustrated, bored, or anxious if you repeat the same maneuver over and over and over.

Back through the pattern to the corner.

Use a left leg cue to ask the horse to move her hip to the right, and a left neck-rein cue to move her head and shoulders to the left.

Back out of the obstacle.

CENTERING YOUR HORSE TO PREPARE TO BACK

Finally, you must teach the horse to set up in the correct starting position. Your goal is to have the horse perfectly centered between the poles. In tough competition, these small details will count toward the winning score. Your approach and position in relation to the poles can make this easy or difficult. If you are too far from the poles, it will be more difficult to put the horse in the proper position. Always set yourself up for success. Learn your horse's easiest and best position at the beginning of the back-up, and then aim to put him there if the pattern allows.

Walk your horse at right angles to the start of the back-up. Stop and let your horse relax. Teaching him to wait for your cue to proceed will pay dividends in the show ring. If ever he begins to anticipate the back up and starts to maneuver into position without your cue, return to this beginning position and force him to stand quietly and wait. Then walk off without performing the back-through. Change his mind. A brief rest or hesitation during training should prevent him from forming the habit of rushing through the back-up.

The first method is to use the same type of ninety-degree turn that you used to make the L-shaped turn discussed above. Your horse pivots around the imaginary pole running through his withers. His hindquarters turn to the left as his front end swings to the right, or vice versa, depending on which side of the obstacle you start.

Stop your horse when your leg is in the middle of the back-up. Fine tune the distance until you can pivot your horse and set him up correctly between the poles. Leave enough room from the top of the poles so that the horse will not step on, bump, or tip the poles as he swings his hips into place. With most horses, this will be a foot or two in front of the poles. As you practice, you will find the right distance to set him up close but without bumping the poles.

Remember, if you ask your horse to make the turn too far from the poles, you will have farther to back to put him into position. Also, if you are too far from the poles, the horse may not understand where he is to go and you will have to direct him without benefit of the outline made by the poles. If you wiggle and squiggle in the saddle, looking to see if your horse is in the right position, you could inadvertently cue your horse without realizing it. Then the horse will move left and right trying to obey your cues. You get mad, not realizing that it is your antics in the saddle that are cueing the horse.

Instead, make the turn to line your horse up with the obstacle and take a quick glance at the pole (either to your left or right) as you begin to back-through. If you see that you are in line with the pole on the left, I promise you that the opposite (right) pole is also in line with your horse. From practicing at home you should have memorized how much of the twenty-eight inches to thirty inches between poles is left. You don't need to look at both poles. It will just give you one more chance to inadvertently cue your horse.

Another method you can use to set your horse in the correct position is to stop with his hind leg in line with the path of your planned back-up route. For example, if you walk towards an L-shaped back-through with the poles on your left, you should

1. First, walk your horse forward through the poles.

2. Then back out. Twisting in the saddle will cause your horse to step out or bump the poles.

stop with the horse's right hind leg one third past the first pole and two thirds before the last pole. Cue your horse to perform a ninety-degree turn. In other words, your horse should plant the right hind leg in the ground and, keeping his body straight from head to tail, sweep his entire body to the right ninety degrees. After he makes the turn he should end up evenly between the two poles. As you practice, you will learn exactly where you must stop to put your horse in the correct position.

3. To set your horse up between the poles at the start of the back-out, walk over the corner of the pole nearest you.

4. Proceed slowly, one step at a time.

5. When the horse has crossed the pole with his back feet, use your right leg to push his hip left and your reins to guide his head and shoulders right until he is square between the poles.

6. Back a step or two and stop.

7. Then back out. Teach your horse to wait for your cue.

Look left . . .

. . . or right, to see if you are lined up with the poles, but do not twist in the saddle.

As you begin to back the length of the poles, sit up, look ahead and only glance with your eyes to be sure that the pole is still in line with your horse. If you move your head so much that it moves your shoulders, that can cause you to move your hands and therefore your reins or your legs, cueing the horse out of position.

Out of the corner of your eye you will see the horse approaching the corner of the "L." At that point, ask the horse to move his hip to the right with a left leg cue. Simultaneously, ask him to move his front end to the left with a right neck rein cue. Once he has made the turn (and again you must rely on looking at the poles out of the corner of your eye so that you don't over-cue the horse), ask him to back the final straight segment. Back completely out of the "L"—a step or two past the end of the poles. When at a show, be sure to allow enough room to maneuver to the next obstacle.

VARIATIONS OF THE BACK-THROUGH

After you have mastered entering and then making the turn in an L-shaped back-up, use the same principle and apply it to the other back-up obstacles. Backing through the "U" or "V" follows the same method except the turns are slightly different. The "U" requires that you make two turns to back out in the same direction from which you entered the obstacle. The "V" back-through is similar to the "L," but requires a tighter turn. Some of the junior classes at small, open shows only ask the contestants to back a straight pattern. But, if you practice on the more demanding obstacles, your horse should master the easier ones readily.

Besides the serpentine and "L" back-up obstacles, a pattern might ask you to back around three cones outlined by poles to make a trickier and tighter obstacle. Set up three cones in a triangle shape. The top two cones should be twenty-eight to thirty-six inches apart, with the third cone at the bottom of the triangle the same distance away. If this obstacle is outlined by poles, the poles must be three to four feet from the cones. Your horse may not step over nor bump into the poles. If you drew your backing steps on paper, it would look like the bottom of a light bulb. Practice backing through this obstacle, maintaining control as you back step by step.

As your horse becomes comfortable with backing, you can ask him to back through an elevated obstacle. Raise the poles twelve inches from the ground. Be sure they are firmly in place and will not tumble if your horse taps them as he backs. When he masters the twelve-inch elevation, raise it to twenty-one inches. Elevated poles are often easier for your horse to negotiate than you might imagine. They outline his path and provide guidelines to follow. But you still need to practice so that he becomes comfortable with the elevated obstacles. Never leave anything to chance.

You can practice backing between and through cones, or zigzag and serpentine through them. When you make a turn that is less than a ninety-degree angle, as is in the "L"-back-up, you will use your legs to guide the horse more than you use the reins. As you practice, monitor the amount and placement of leg and rein pressure to which your horse best responds and work to fine tune it.

Once you have maneuverability and control in your back-up, set up the poles or markers at the minimum distance, or even a little closer together. If your horse can maneuver through tight cones, the wider spacing at a show will be easy.

Continue to work on your horse's maneuverability in reverse as part of his routine training, but don't overdo to the point that he gets sick of backing around, or through, obstacles. Try to soften or lighten your rein cue as much as possible. Work on sitting and looking straight ahead. Your seat should remain squarely in the saddle so that you do not inadvertently cue your horse. Be prepared to find some type of back-up in each and every trail class that you enter. A back-up is a mandatory obstacle. With practice, guiding in reverse should become no harder than guiding your horse forward.

STOP ANTICIPATION IN ITS TRACKS

When practicing at home you should stop your horse at any point through the "L," hesitate and then back a few steps. Your horse must learn to sit and wait, especially if he tends to rush through the obstacle. Patience is a virtue! Stop your horse halfway through the backing obstacle and then walk forward out of it. If your horse doesn't want to stop, bump him forward with a hard heel cue. Use the bump as a correction. It says to a horse, "No! No! No! You must pay attention to what I am asking you." Your goal is to keep your horse waiting for you to tell him what to do or where to go next. Don't let him anticipate. The best way to stop anticipation is to never let a horse learn that he can move without your cue. If your horse tries to back up without a cue, bump him forward and make him walk out of the obstacle. Change his mind. Stay one step ahead of your horse's thinking. Be a rider, not a passenger.

EIGHT

SIDEPASSING

By now, your horse should understand to move away from leg pressure. He will flex at the poll and give to the bit in response to rein pressure. You can use your aids to control his head, hips, and shoulders. You must have these tools at your disposal to teach your horse even the simplest of obstacles. Teaching a horse to sidepass gets him moving away from leg pressure cue in the initial stages of training. Later it is used to sidepass over an obstacle, perhaps in a "W" or "L" formation. Your horse must sidepass to allow you to open or close a gate. You can also utilize the sidepass

to correct your positioning. For example, if you are too far from or to close to an obstacle, you can sidepass either left or right to correct your horse's position in relation to it.

LEARNING THE SIDEPASS

Start this lesson by working on the maneuvers you learned in the previous chapters. Ask your horse to bend around your inside leg, getting him to move away from leg pressure. The same exercise will reinforce that he must flex at the poll and give to the

A horse must sidepass to negotiate the gate.

To begin the sidepass, lift your reins to halt forward motion. Do not use so much pressure that your horse backs. Notice the cross-over step in back.

Followed by the cross-over step in front.

bit in response to rein pressure. As he becomes proficient in those skills, ask him to counter-bend between the cones, (real or imaginary) in your work area. This forms the basis for the sidepass maneuver. At this point in time, you should begin to feel that you have some control over your horse's forward and lateral movement. He may not be finely tuned, but his mouth should have the beginning of that soft, buttery feeling and he should respond when you apply your leg to his side. If you do not get a response, continue to work on the circling maneuvers and progress to the counter-bending maneuver before asking him to sidepass. These skills will help him to sidepass, as well as become more maneuverable through the other trail course obstacles.

I usually put about sixty days of training into an unbroken colt before I begin to sidepass or work the various obstacles. Some youngsters take as long as four months, while a very few will be ready in a month. If you are training an older horse that is already broken to ride, he may learn these skills quicker. It will vary from horse to horse, and also depending upon how often you ride and your degree of skill. Don't get discouraged. Your horse will learn to sidepass on his timetable. It is not as difficult as your horse might try to make you believe. If you run into problems, read the section on trouble shooting. A horse does not travel sideways naturally. You are asking him to be obedient to your aids and to obey a command that is unnatural for him. You must reward him for trying in the initial stages. If he takes one sideways step, release all aids and reward him, so that he will understand what it is that you are asking of him. Later, you may ask for several sideways steps.

When your horse has worked off his excess energy and is ready to settle down and pay attention, begin to work on this lesson. To teach a sidepass to the right, first walk two or three small circles to the left, bending him around your inside left leg. The smallness of the circle forces the horse

Sidepassing over a pole.

Horses must be taught to move away from leg pressure. It is not a natural response for them. (Untrained horses push against pressure.) My right leg pressure cues this mare to sidepass to the left.

to throw his hindquarters outside the circle to the right. While this is not a truly correct circle in the sense of what you would be asked to do in a dressage test, use it as a training aid to help the horse understand he is to move his hindquarters away from leg pressure. Walk two to three small circles. Then let him out of the circle and walk straight ahead for ten or twenty feet. Next, ask for two or three more circles, remembering to bend him around your inside leg. Work on just one side at first.

Stop and pick up the reins just enough so that your horse cannot walk forward. Do not use so much rein pressure that he backs. This is the second component of the sidepass. You must learn to adjust the amount of rein pressure to keep your horse from walking forward but not enough pressure to cause him to back. This applies whether your horse is learning to sidepass or is a seasoned campaigner. The side pass is controlled through both hand and leg aids. Learn to adjust the pressure to suit your horse on any

She lifts her front leg, preparing to cross over.

given day. If he begins to walk forward, use a little more rein pressure. If he tries to back up, use a little less.

To ask for the sidepass, hold your horse's head between your hands and apply your left leg at the girth. The reins keep him from moving forward

At some shows you might be required to sidepass first left . . .

. . . and then right.

forward or try to turn. Giving light sideways rein pressure will help some horses understand they should move their shoulders over.

When the horse takes one step, or even the suggestion of a side step, you must immediately release all pressure and praise him. Your goal is to convey to the horse that he did a great thing by taking that one sideways step. Let him relax for a minute to think about it. Then ask for another step. Praise and ask for a third step. Three times is enough. Do not drill over and over. Stop asking, so that your horse understands that he did what you requested. The release of pressure, or in this case ceasing to ask for the maneuver, rewards the horse. Work on other maneuvers or walk, jog and lope for five to ten minutes before asking again on the same side in the same direction. Again, work on something unrelated to sidepassing and then start the process all over on the opposite side.

The unrelated work you make the horse do between switching from one side to the other "changes a horse's mind." He switches from thinking "sidepass to the left" to thinking of "move forward." Then, when you begin on the opposite side, the horse can think "sidepass to the right." Without this change between sides, a horse's mind could become "stuck" on the previous maneuver. In this case, his mind would still be on the sidepass to the left. This is just one of the little tricks that make training easier and less stressful. Ask for three steps on the new side, change and work on something else, and then ask again. After this last repetition , do not ask for any more sidepasses for the day. Repeat the entire procedure tomorrow.

Your horse may surprise you and easily give you two steps. Praise him for doing so, but don't try to see how many steps you can get. Remember, a

or to either side (thus the term "holding his head between your hands"). Keep your hands above the horse's withers, not below his neck. If your horse chooses to move only his hips to the right, apply a light sideways pressure with the right direct rein (still holding the reins evenly to stop forward motion). This will unlock his shoulders and help him understand that he is to move his shoulders as well as his hindquarters. This gets a little tricky. Keep enough even tension on the reins so the horse doesn't walk trail horse must learn to move step by step on command. Don't rush him now. It will be harder to slow him down later. Be patient and ask for just one step at a time. It will not take long before he will understand it completely and you'll appreciate having proceeded slowly.

Of course, a trail horse will often be asked to sidepass first one way and then the other at a show. But training takes time, and you will do more harm than good by rushing in the initial stages. Be patient. Let your horse learn at his own pace. Eventually you will have a solidly broke horse that can and will do whatever you ask of him with a minimum of fuss. He will understand your aids or cues and therefore will not be resentful or frustrated.

If you ride the horse five times a week, wait a minimum of two weeks before asking for a sidepass (even one step) to the left immediately followed by a step to the right. It will not hurt to wait even longer to avoid confusion. Training takes time. Training for trail requires that you teach the horse to stay calm and quiet. Never rush. Take what you get each day and build on it each succeeding day. Teach your horse to enjoy the slowness and correctness of trail. Do not try to drill the sidepass maneuver into his head in one day. You will only confuse him and create problems.

TROUBLE SHOOTING

If you cannot get your horse to sidepass because he walks forward through your reins, walk him up to a fence or any solid wall so that it stops his forward motion. Hold your hands in the same way you would without a fence, so that he learns your cues. Hold his head between your hands, keeping it aligned with his body. Do not let your horse evade your leg cue to sidepass by turning his entire body and walking to the side. Hold his head facing the fence and apply your leg cue. Ask him to sidepass (either to the left or to the right). If he takes one step, release your aids and praise him. Ask again on the same side. Remember, before you ask him to sidepass in the other direction, you must walk around the arena to change his mind. Once he learns to sidepass facing the fence, on succeeding days you can gradually move farther away from it before you ask for a sidepass. Continue increasing the distance until he no longer relies on the fence to stop his forward motion.

Now ask your horse to sidepass in the opposite direction. At this point some horses will try to sidepass in the direction that you originally taught them. They seem to think that because you praised them for going in one direction they can be rewarded again for sidepassing in that direction, regardless of your cues. In this case, apply a stronger leg cue or help the horse with a rein cue. Praise when he gets it right. Reward. Rest. Repeat.

Never overwork this exercise on the first day. Remember that "What you teach a horse today, he learns tomorrow." Ask for a few steps today and reward your horse for doing well. Then either dismount or go on to different work.

If your horse will sidepass in one direction but not in the other, place him in a corner. The fence to the front will block his forward motion and the fence to the side will block sideways motion. Use your legs to bump him forward if he tries to back. This leaves only one option—to sidepass in the direction that you asked.

Actually, the cues you use to ask a horse to sidepass employ a similar process. Your reins block the horse's forward motion, creating a "door"

If you are having trouble, stand facing a fence to stop your horse's forward motion.

Notice the cross-over step in front.

The mare's body has gotten out of line, so I use more right rein pressure to slow her shoulders and front legs, and more right leg to speed up her back legs until she is straight again.

through which he cannot pass. Your leg pressure cue to move sideways (sidepass) blocks your horse from moving in one direction. Therefore, the only option "open" to the horse is to move sideways in the opposite direction, away from your leg pressure. That is why you must be sure to take the opposite leg off his side—it gives him an "open" place to go. Remember this theory as you train. You block the various parts of the horse's body with your leg and rein cues. However, you must leave him an open door as the correct place to move.

If you cannot teach your horse from his back what you want, then ask your horse to sidepass from the ground. Apply pressure with your hand at the same point on his side where your leg would cue him if you were mounted. Push him over. When he willingly moves from your hand on the ground, mount and ask again using the leg cue. If he still does not seem to understand, employ the help of an assistant. Ask this person to apply pressure from the ground in the exact same spot that you used to teach him to move away from your hand. If he moves one step, praise him to let him know that he did the right thing, and then ask again. Continue in this manner. Ask from his back and rely less and less on your assistant's help from the ground.

Most horses learn from the first method, but it does take a degree of feel on your part to know how much rein and leg to use. Continue to work on feeling how much pressure to apply. Just as your horse will learn given enough time, you will develop this feel if you work at it.

EXAGGERATE IN THE BEGINNING

Keep in mind that aids often must be exaggerated in the beginning. The more clear, concise and consistent your aids, the quicker your horse will learn. Once he understands that the new cue you are teaching means something, you can lighten up that cue and your horse will still respond.

Remember: a stressed or nervous horse will not learn as readily as a calm, quiet horse. Neither can you become frustrated. You must be patient, just like a first grade teacher. Use whatever "language" it takes until your horse understands. Keep asking and trying and you will teach him.

When your horse will sidepass one step, add a second step. Add a third step after he learns to take two steps, and so forth. When he has progressed to taking four or five sideways steps, you can begin to position him over a pole and ask him to sidepass a step or two over it. Reward him by a brief rest. Repeat, and stop halfway down the length of the pole. Resting will teach the horse not to worry about the pole under him. Stopping also will prevent him from thinking that he must sidepass the entire length of the pole before you ask. Teach your horse to wait for your cues, especially as you begin to negotiate obstacles such as the "W."

BUILDING THE "W"

After you master a basic sidepass, you can begin to work on the more difficult maneuvers. I will give detailed directions on side passing the "W," but you can modify this to an "L," a "V," or any number of other sidepass maneuvers. After your horse understands the aids used for the basic sidepass, it is fairly easy to add the turn on the forehand and turn on the haunches needed to perform the more complicated maneuvers.

I build the "W" out of heavy logs. If a horse bumps these heavy poles, in most cases he will be more careful not to bump them the next time. Heavy logs don't shift out of place as easily as light ones so you won't need to dismount to readjust them if your horse strikes them. However, if light logs or jump poles are all that are available, go ahead and use them. Later it is advisable to practice over white or striped poles such as the ones used at shows, regardless of the type of pole you used initially.

When beginning to school a horse over this obstacle, I use long, solid poles to make it as easy as I can for the horse. I want him to learn how to maneuver through the obstacles and to gain the confidence that he can maneuver through them. Starting with an obstacle that is beyond the horse's ability at any given time can scare him and set back his training. Using long, solid poles allows me to open up the "W" so that the horse does not trip on the next pole or become confused by two poles laying close together. The length allows me to stop the horse and make him wait for my cue to continue. I have time to make minor adjustments to his body position if, for example, he begins to lead with his shoulder rather than keep his body straight. Of course, if you use the longer poles, your horse needs to be able to perform the sidepass really well before you attempt the "W."

SIDEPASSING THE "W"

When your horse is comfortable with sidepassing over one pole on the ground, progress to the "W." Position your horse at the beginning of the "W" (top of the left pole, facing right in this example), loosen your reins and sit still for a few minutes. This will keep your horse from rushing down the pole as soon as you set him up. Horses are creatures of habit and will soon learn that a pole under their belly means to sidepass the length of it. This can create a problem because in some classes you may be asked to perform a different maneuver. A horse that has not been taught to wait will be down the pole before you can count to three. Try to make this obstacle an enjoyable place to be rather than something to "get over with." Get your horse to relax and wait for your cue by sitting

Leg pressure *at the girth* tells a horse to move his entire body sideways.
Leg pressure *behind the girth* tells him to move only his hind end.

quietly on his back and letting him enjoy the reward of a rest. You can do this before you start, and also when he is halfway down the pole.

Ask your horse to sidepass to the right down the length of the first pole, until he reaches the bottom of the "W," where the two poles meet. (Note: If ever you feel your horse is rushing, stop halfway down the length of the pole and rest. If he continues to rush,

stop part way, rest for a moment, and then walk forward over the pole and start again at the beginning.)

Your horse must do a turn on the forehand in order to make the corner of the "W." His front feet stay in place as his hindquarters swing around his forelegs in a half circle. To push your horse's hindquarters to the right, apply left leg pressure behind the girth. His hind end will swing to the right around the logs as his front legs pivot in place.Lift your hand slightly to steady his head and to tell him not to walk forward. In the initial stages, using one hand on each rein will help you to keep the horse's head and shoulders steady and in place.

After your horse has made the turn on the forehand around the bottom of the "W," his body should be positioned in a straight line and ready to sidepass the second pole. Before you ask him to sidepass the second pole, let him stop and stand. Sit relaxed on his back and count to fifty. You want the horse to learn to wait for your cue before moving. Sing a song, recite poetry or anything you can think of while the horse stands quietly positioned over the log. Make him wait until you tell him to sidepass the next pole. This will teach him not to anticipate. It also helps to make him think that this maneuver is enjoyable—he gets to rest. In the training stage, resting also gives him time to absorb the steps that he just completed.

Now, ask him to sidepass the second pole. Do this in the same way that you asked for the sidepass over the first pole, using the same sequence of cues. When you come to the next corner, your horse must perform a turn on the haunches. His hindquarters remain in place while his front legs perform a half circle. This is similar to a spin, except the horse does not plant his hind pivot foot in the ground. His

1. Starting the "W."

2. Sidepass the first pole.

3. Push the horse's hips around the corner to get lined up with the second pole.

4. Sidepass the second pole.

5. Hold the horse's hind end in place as his front end moves around the corner.

6. Sidepass the third pole.

hind feet can take baby steps as he moves his front legs and shoulders around the turn.

Instead of using your leg to ask the horse to move, use a rein cue to direct his front feet in a half circle to the right. Hold your right leg lightly at the girth to keep the horse's hindquarters still as he turns his forehand to the right to make the corner. If you try to push a horse's forequarters around a turn with your legs (as you would in a spin), you will probably confuse him. He might plant his pivot foot and step over the log with a hind foot. The horse must finish the turn with his body lined up straight with the next pole and ready to sidepass it.

With your horse's body positioned correctly over the third pole, stop and rest as before. Then, ask him to sidepass over the third pole. At the last corner or angle, do another turn on the forehand (the same as the first) and stop again. Line your horse up correctly with the last pole and sidepass it. Sit quietly at the last pole and praise your horse for a tough maneuver well done.

With a young or green trail horse, practice just the sidepass and turn on the forehand for a few days or weeks. Stop him over the poles and let him rest. Then walk forward over the pole and out. Repeat. As he gains proficiency at this segment of the maneuver, add the sidepass and turn on the haunches. Only when your horse has shown by his calm acceptance of both these maneuvers should you ask for the entire "W." If your horse seems anxious or tries to anticipate your cues, stop him, sit on his back, and let him rest. If you are calm, your horse will be calm. If you are nervous, your horse will feel it and become nervous too. Horses react to a rider that is nervous, angry, scared, or frustrated and will want to hurry through the obstacle.

THE CURE FOR RUSHING

If an older, trained horse begins to anticipate or rush through an obstacle, teach him that a set of poles on the ground does not always mean to sidepass a "W." They may mean to jog through the poles or sidepass an "L." To cure him of anticipating, ask him to sidepass the first pole to the right and then back in the opposite direction, to the left. Ask the horse to sidepass half of a log, then step over the log and walk away. Come back to the obstacle and sidepass a different log. Return to the obstacle at the end of your lesson and work a portion of it. Then ask your horse to stop. Dismount right there and walk away. Do anything that you can to change the obstacle and make the horse wait for your directions. He must learn that you tell him when to move and you tell him what direction to move.

Teaching your horse to perform this demanding maneuver (which incorporates a sidepass, a turn on the forehand, and a turn on the haunches), will help your horse to become more flexible and supple throughout his body. He will also become more obedient and learn to wait for and to obey your cues. You will gain skill in moving your horse's head, hips, and shoulders. If you can master the toughest obstacles with ease, the simpler obstacles should be a breeze.

OTHER SIDEPASS OBSTACLES

Simpler variations of the sidepass include, but are not limited to, sidepassing a single pole on the ground. At other times that pole may be elevated to a maximum height of twelve inches. Be sure the pole is positioned under your stirrup when you

7. Sidepass the fourth pole.

8. Stop at the end and praise your horse.

start to sidepass, and keep it there for the duration of the obstacle. Also, make certain that the elevated pole is set in such a way that it will not roll if your horse bumps it.

You may be asked to sidepass between two poles placed on the ground. The poles may be spaced no closer than twenty to twenty-four inches apart. Either the horse's front or back feet will be in between the poles as he sidepasses their length. Again, put the pole under your stirrup and sidepass in a straight line. Sit straight, look straight, and cue your horse to sidepass. If you wiggle in the saddle, checking to see where the pole is, you will inadvertently cue your horse and cause him to bump the pole. That will cause you to lose points off your score. Trust your horse's ability to do his job. Learn to feel if he is straight or if he is moving forwards or backwards.

WATCH THE WAY YOU RIDE

If your horse has a tendency to bump the pole in a sidepass—or any obstacle—as you progress with his training, check the way you ride. Your horse may be performing as you direct! Ask a friend to watch or videotape your ride. Purposely wiggle in the saddle once to learn why you must sit straight. Often a rider will cue a horse in this manner without realizing that he is giving conflicting cues. Watch what happens to your hands and legs as you turn left or right. You will see why your horse hits the poles when you move. It is because when you lean over to look to the left, you will often hit the horse in the side with your left leg and cue him to move to the right. Your right hand on the reins might apply a right neckrein cue because you shift your hand to the left as you look left, and visa versa. Do not to look down at the pole. Your horse will place his feet where you look. Sit up. Look ahead. Sit centered in the saddle. Help your horse to balance and perform the obstacles with ease by sitting quietly and allowing him to do his job.

NINE

GATES

THE GATE is usually a mandatory obstacle included in every pattern. It may be the first obstacle of a pattern, in which case performing it well will give a judge a good first impression. It can be the last obstacle, allowing your horse to finish the pattern with brilliance or gain points lost elsewhere in the pattern. The gate is also found in the middle of a trail pattern. There is no set rule. Because it is mandatory, you want your horse to do well on this obstacle. In this chapter, we will cover how to train your horse to work both a rope gate and a wooden gate.

When your horse will reliably sidepass from your leg cue, you can teach him to work a gate. It is easier if the horse will neck rein. However, in the beginning stages you can help him with a direct rein if needed (such as when making the sharp turn around the gate after opening it). If you followed the program in this book, you have already taught your horse to bend around your inside leg. That cue will help him bend his middle sharply around the end of the gate (after you push it open). This puts him in position to sidepass and push the gate closed. He must make a tight turn around the gate. If the turn is not tight, your horse will have to sidepass farther to push it closed. The fewer side-

passing steps the horse makes to close the gate, the easier it will be for him to perform the maneuver.

TEACH AND USE A CUE TO STAND STILL

Learning a verbal "Whoa!" command will help your horse to maneuver through the gate. It allows you to concentrate on opening the gate rather than halting the horse. When first learning this maneuver, a horse will often continue walking forward after they are through the gate, rather than stopping in a position where you can close it easily. This may happen because the horse is unsure of how to maneuver around the gate. He may get nervous and want to walk away. Another horse would prefer to move on, rather than wait for the next cue to move. In any case, teaching a horse to obey the verbal command, "Whoa," is useful in the initial training stage. After enough repetitions, your horse will maneuver through the gate without the verbal whoa command. You should not use a verbal "Whoa" during an actual show.

If he will not stand willingly on a verbal whoa, you can teach your horse an additional command to stand still.

65

Push your rein hand into his neck every time you stop beside an obstacle and say the word whoa. Push hard enough that the horse feels your hand, but not so much that it causes discomfort. Keep your hand centered over the horse's neck, pulling the reins neither left nor right. When you prepare to ask him to move, lift your hand prior to asking the horse to move forward. Every time that you want your horse to stop and stand, push your hand into his neck. Consistency is the key! Eventually the horse will feel the slight shift in weight as your hand moves down towards his neck and he will stand without your hand actually touching his neck. After enough repetitions, the suggestion of putting your hand close to his neck will cue the horse to stand still. In other words, you will refine the cue from an exaggerated push to just the suggestion of moving your hand nearer his neck. After a time your horse may no longer need this additional cue, but it can be very helpful initially.

If your horse becomes nervous at an obstacle, even at a show, putting your hand close to his neck just might save the day. With many horses, the use of a cue that they know well and which they will not confuse easily with any other cue, can override the nervousness they feel. In a trail class you cannot touch the horse with either hand, but you can shift your hand and weight to suggest the push of your hand on the horse's neck. This gives the horse a reminder that he should stand still and wait.

If your horse shows nervousness or hesitation when he is close to a new obstacle, spend a few minutes sitting quietly on your horse's back next to that obstacle at the end of a lesson. Then dismount and put the horse up. When you begin the next day's lesson, after your horse is warmed up and ready to work, he should be more relaxed around the obstacle. You can use this concept when teaching a horse to work the gate. If the horse is unsure about working the gate at first, stand your horse by the gate at the end of your lesson, relax and rest for a few minutes. Then dismount. On the second day, open the gate and make the turn to position your horse correctly outside the gate. Dismount after sitting quietly a few minutes. On the third day, ask the horse to sidepass to push the gate closed. Stand by the gate for a few minutes to reward him, dismount and put him away. After the third day, ask the horse to work the entire gate in one lesson. Some horses will usually work the gate willingly from this point onward. Teach the three steps separately and give your horse as much time as he needs to master the entire gate exercise.

THE ROPE GATE

One of the obstacles seen more and more frequently in trail classes is a rope gate rather than a standard wooden or metal gate. It is easier to move to the correct place in the pattern and easier to set up. It is also safer to work. Because the actual gate is made of a rope, there is less chance for a horse to get hurt. Dropping a rope will seldom cause a horse to spook. Letting a wooden gate swing in the breeze can sometimes spook a horse. Set up a practice rope gate at home as your assurance that your horse will understand when faced with one at a show. Usually, though, a well-broke horse will handle the demands of a rope gate as easily, if not easier, than the old type wooden gate.

Building a rope gate at home is quite simple—much easier, in fact, than building a wooden gate. If you happen to be involved in jumping, you can borrow two jump standards to use as uprights for your rope gate. Simply tie a rope at the top of one standard. Space the two standards six to eight feet apart (the same distance apart as the rope.) Make a loop at the other end of the rope to fasten over the top of the second jump standard to "close" the gate.

If you must build uprights to use for your rope gate, purchase two treated (they last longer) four-by-four boards six feet long. You also need eight eighteen-inch pieces of two-by-six boards. Nail a two-by-six to each of the four sides of the bottom of the four-by-four poles. This forms a base of support as shown in the photos.

Working the Rope Gate

To begin teaching the rope gate, walk your horse parallel to the gate and stop when your knee is at the "handle" (loop of rope that you must lift to "open" the gate). Depending on the level of your horse's training, you can either walk him directly next to the gate to lift the loop, or you can start a few feet to the side of the gate and sidepass to the correct position to reach the loop.

If you stop too far forward or behind the loop handle, you will have to move your horse a few steps forward or backward until your hand is lined up with the loop. Your goal when showing is to put your horse in the proper position on the first try. The fewer steps your horse makes in this "dance" the less opportunity there is for a mistake. However, when practicing, always make those forward or backward steps to line up with the handle so your horse learns the proper position. Then, if it becomes necessary at a show, he will have practiced the maneuver. If your horse will will-

ingly, calmly, and correctly move where you put him, you will not lose points as you will by zigzagging left or right or leaning over to reach the handle. If you drastically shift your weight, you might also move your rein hand or apply a leg cue without being aware of it. Your goal is to present a polished, professional, picture. That takes practice. As you're schooling, polish your approach until you get it right.

When your horse is in the correct position for you to easily lift the loop of the gate, ask your horse to stand for a moment or two. Do not go on to the gate maneuver. Make the horse stand and wait for your cues. A common problem is that horses learn to anticipate. They learn how to maneuver through a gate and will do so without your cue. It's important to teach your horse right from the beginning that he must move step by step on your command. Teaching him to wait for your cue is vital to preventing anticipation.

Once your horse is standing quietly and relaxed beside the handle of the gate, lift the loop and make him wait another minute or two. Then back a step or two. He must have room for his front end to cross to the opposite side of the gate (behind the upright that held the gate handle). After he takes a step or two backwards, stop him and wait again. You must have patience to teach your horse not to anticipate or rush.

With a left-hand gate (your left hand is on the rope and your horse is on the right side of the gate), back a step or two as mentioned above. Then, turn your horse sharply to the left to pass through the "opening" between the two uprights. Do not let go of the rope. Turn your horse 180-degrees to the left so he is once again parallel with the gate, but facing in the opposite direction. Stop and wait again.

1. Build wooden gateposts with a stand made of crossed two-by-six boards to hold them.

2. Set your horse up correctly so you don't have to reach for the latch. This rider is reaching too far.

3. Lift up the loop and back a few steps.

4. Turn to go through the gate.

5. Complete the turn, maintaining control of the rope.

6. Back a step and then drop the loop over the gatepost.

Relax. When your horse is calm and quiet, back him a few steps so that you are in position to latch the gate. If your horse tries to throw his hip to the right (away from the upright), keep your outside (right) leg on him as you back those few steps so that he cannot swing away from the gate. Know your horse. Does it take a lot of leg pressure to hold him in place or just a slight touch? Find what works.

When your hand is even with the upright where you will hang the loop, stop your horse and "close" the gate. Let your horse stand quietly here and praise him for a job well done. Be sure that you ask the horse to move off. Do not let him choose when to move. When training, always make your horse wait for your next command.

If you are showing, of course, you omit the long rest periods between each step of the obstacle. At a show, when you complete an obstacle, look for the next obstacle, get your bearings and then move on. Don't rush. Take your time and be sure both you and your horse are ready before you proceed.

If at any point your horse begins to rush while maneuvering through a gate, ask him to stop at that point. Sit quietly to show him there is nothing to fear and no reason to rush. If that doesn't improve your horse's behavior, there are a few correction methods that may help. If your older horse is the type that likes to get quick and move around rather than stand still, show him it is to his benefit to enjoy his reward of a rest. Ask him to stand once more. If he continues to move around or dance in place, make him lope around the arena enough to get him slightly winded, tired, and thinking of stopping. Immediately bring him back to that segment of the gate and ask him to stand. If he moves around, lope him again. Wait until he

If you get too far from the post you may lose the gate.

shows signs of wanting to stop, then make him lope another minute or two before you allow him to stop. Bring him back to the gate. You may need to repeat this correction three or four times until the horse learns that his options are either to stand still and relax or to work hard and lope. He will soon learn that it is to his benefit to stand still when asked.

On the other hand, if a horse is afraid of the gate, I bring the horse as close as I can to the gate and ask him to stand. When the horse settles and stands quietly, I pet his neck, dismount and put him away. Dismounting is a big reward for a horse and ending your lesson by the gate makes him think of the gate as a nice place to be. This method is helpful for a timid horse that worries about being too close to an obstacle.

If you have ridden a horse quietly up to the point of gate training and taught him to sidepass and to stop and wait for your cues before he moves, it may only take a week to teach a young horse how to maneuver correctly through a gate. However, if

1. Unlatch the gate.

2. Back a couple of steps so your horse can maneuver through the opening.

3. Push the gate open. Be sure to maintain control of the gate! Don't take your hand off while showing, although when training, remember—safety first.

4. Walk through the opening. Keep the opening slightly wider than your horse, but not so wide that you have to make extra steps to close the gate.

5. Turn sharply around the gate, making a 180-degree turn.

you have an older horse that is quick and dislikes standing still, you must go back and reestablish control, correctness, and slowness. He must learn to wait for your cue before moving, and he must learn to stand still until told otherwise.

THE SOLID GATE

To begin to work a wooden or metal gate, walk your horse parallel to the gate with the gate on your right side (we will use a right-hand gate for this example). Stop your horse when your knee is at the latch of the gate, or when you are positioned so that you can easily reach the latch. With a horse that is completely trustworthy at sidepassing, you can stay a few feet to the left of the gate handle and sidepass one or two steps to the right to the correct position. If your horse has not progressed that far in his training, walk parallel beside the gate.

When your horse is in position, open the gate and back your horse a step or two parallel with the gate, keeping your hand on the gate. You will be penalized for loosing control of

6. Sidepass to shut the gate.

7. Back a few steps until you are in position to latch the gate.

the gate. Push the gate open to the right (for a right hand, push gate) to give your horse enough room to maneuver through the opening. Walk through the gate and turn your horse sharply 180-degrees to the right to face the other direction. You must be sure that the gate doesn't poke the horse in the side as you make the turn. Because you pushed the gate open to maneuver your horse through the gate, you'll now ask your horse to sidepass to push the gate closed. In the initial stages, push the gate over a little away from the horse with your hand so the horse has room to sidepass without walking into the gate. As he learns this maneuver, the horse will be more relaxed with the gate close to his side. Push the gate closed. Back a few steps so that you are in position to latch the

gate. If your horse tries to throw his hip to the right (away from the gate), keep your outside leg on him as you back so that he cannot swing away. When your hand is even with where the gate latches, stop your horse and close the gate. Make your horse stand quietly before moving again. Make him wait for your cue to move.

Remember to take your time and go step by step. A trail class is not timed. A slow and correct horse will be scored higher than a horse that works the gate fast but makes mistakes. Do not stop the horse between each segment of gate work when you are at a show. Simply ask your horse to go slowly as you taught him at home. Use your leg and rein cues to guide him through the maneuver. Speed him up if he tries to lag or stop. Slow him down if he tries to rush. Don't allow your horse to take over the reins of control and work the gate the way he wants. He must obey your cues if you want to make a polished, professional appearance that keeps you from "getting" the gate.

Your goal for the maximum allowable points is a horse that will calmly negotiate the gate. You do not want to set a record for the speediest time, nor do you want the slowest time. You want a horse that presents a quiet, well-mannered picture of absolute trust and willing obedience as he obeys your cues. Strive to manipulate the gate with manners, style, and grace.

If you want a good trail horse, choose one that shows interest in his surroundings, is careful where he places his feet, and has a calm, steady disposition.

TEN

BRIDGES

INTRODUCING A HORSE to a bridge may look deceptively simple to the uninformed. How hard can it be to get a horse to walk over a sheet of plywood or a few boards? However, the horse sees a bridge from a different perspective. A horse's instincts tell him to be careful where he puts his hooves. In some cases, when a horse refuses what seems a simple exercise to the rider, the horse is only following his instincts. A raised bridge makes a hollow sound as the horse's hoofs clippity-clop over it. He will feel a slight give to the boards as his weight hits them. He cannot differentiate between an actual bridge and a sheet of plywood or fake bridge. He will probably be apprehensive about any type of bridge at first. Teach your horse that he must go forward on your command and trust your judgment. He should obey your cues to go forward, whether or not he agrees with your reasoning. Remember: never abuse that trust and scare a horse with an obstacle that is beyond his ability at any given point in time.

CROSSING A SIMPLE BRIDGE

To train your horse to cross a bridge, start with a simple sheet of plywood laying flat on the ground. Save the white paint until your horse willingly crosses over the plain sheet of plywood. Some horses will walk over the plain sheet of plywood with barely a second glance, making you wonder why teaching a horse to cross a bridge is such a big deal. Other horses will snort, spook and refuse to put a hoof on anything that even resembles a bridge.

With either type of horse, begin training with a simple sheet of plywood. You will quickly find out what type of horse you own. If your horse has been showing for a number of years and has learned to respect and obeys your cues to go forward, chances are he'll walk over the plywood with barely a glance. If you are starting a young horse, or are training an older horse you've recently acquired, the plywood will give you insight into your horse's willingness to obey a go forward cue.

If your horse calmly walks over the plywood, approach it from either direction a few times and let him walk over it. Then work on something else or put him up for the day. Your goal at this point is to find out what your horse's reaction will be. If he crosses the plywood easily, the other types of bridges probably will not be a problem for him.

Give your horse more rein to encourage him to drop his head and look at the bridge.

Another youth horse shows acceptance of a raised bridge.

However, if your horse refuses to cross the plywood, use the following method. You can also use this method later if your horse will cross a sheet of plywood but will not cross a raised bridge. The training method is the same, whether you are teaching the horse to cross a sheet of plywood or a fancy bright yellow bridge.

WARM UP FIRST

Never take a fresh, energetic horse right out of his stall and attempt to cross a bridge for the first time. Save the bridge lesson for the end of your training session when your horse is settled and ready to pay attention to you. This way you can also reward the horse, whether he crosses the bridge or merely puts a foot on it. When your horse obeys to the best of his ability on that day, you should dismount and put him up, as a reward for a job well done.

Never scare a horse by trying to force him to cross a bridge. You want him to learn that a bridge—flat, raised, or otherwise—is merely one more step in his training regime; something that he must do to earn his oats.

Begin by walking your horse towards the plywood as if it were not even there. As you guide the horse across the center of the plywood bridge, your body language must remain relaxed and calm. If you get tense or nervous, anticipating a refusal or a fight, the horse will interpret this as fear and therefore a perfectly good reason not to cross the bridge. Set yourself up for success by thinking that the horse will walk calmly over the plywood. Anticipate that he will cross the bridge. Don't let your fearful anticipation "tell" him not to cross the bridge. In many cases, if your horse feels that you sincerely expect that he will cross the bridge, he'll step right over it with barely a second thought.

Keep your horse's head "between your hands." This simply means to keep a rein in each hand and maintain slight contact with the bit to guide his head straight towards the bridge. If his head moves to the left, correct the movement with a right direct rein and vice versa. Continue towards the bridge in this manner, squeezing both legs to encourage him

Hold a rein in each hand if needed to keep your horse's nose pointed straight.

Use the reins to keep the horse looking straight at the bridge and your legs to encourage her to move forward.

forward. Ask your horse to move closer, step by step, until he finally puts a hoof on the board. Let him stand with one hoof on the board and praise him. When he settles, encourage him forward again. If he tiptoes over the balance of the bridge, praise him. He found the courage and trust to cross. The first time is usually the hardest.

THE NERVOUS OR FRIGHTENED HORSE

If your horse is nervous about crossing the bridge, stop him as close to the bridge as he is comfortable and let him look at it. When he loses interest and begins to look elsewhere, ask him to take one step closer. Let him stand in this new, closer, spot and look at the bridge. When his attention wanders, ask for one more step forward. Continue in this manner until, hopefully, your horse will walk over the bridge step by step. Allow plenty of time to accomplish this. Don't begin on a day that you are rushed. What you might have accomplished in three days can take three weeks because

Allow her to drop her head to look at the bridge.

you pushed the horse for more than he was ready to give on that day.

On the same note, quitting when a horse is misbehaving will only reinforce his disobedience. He will think that if he is "bad" you will not make him cross the scary bridge. Perhaps he can make you get off sooner, too. Soon he will be begin to carry this behavior over to other exercises. For example, he might try to rear on the opposite side of the arena. After all, he reared at the bridge yesterday and you got off real quickly. This is how many vices start. Always think of how your horse may interpret your actions. Try to not push a situation to the point that a horse feels that he must be bad to "tell" you that he doesn't want to do something. Proceed slowly and easily. Take your time, and enforce correctness and obedience in your daily schooling.

If a horse is extremely nervous or flighty, try to find a point in your training where the horse is standing quietly facing the bridge. Don't push him or allow him to act in a manner that could hurt you. If you can't get your horse close enough to the bridge to put a foot on it, find the point where he is comfortable and stop. Sit there for a few minutes. Then dismount at that spot and put him up to think about it overnight. The next day try to get a little closer. Continue in this manner.

Remember: What we teach a horse today, he learns tomorrow. Make the training procedure easy by asking for a little today and a little more tomorrow.

Many times a horse's inquisitiveness will get the better of him and he will stretch his nose towards the bridge, if not, actually walk over and step on it. He may paw at it. Do not make a big issue out of the bridge, especially after a few days. A horse will do these things if he feels through

your body language that there is nothing to fear. However, if you approach a bridge thinking that your horse will be afraid of the bridge and may not cross it, you are predicting the future. Your horse will feel your apprehension as fear. He cannot differentiate between your fear of the bridge and your fear that he will not cross it. All he feels is fear, and that tells him not to cross the bridge. The easiest way to ask a horse to cross a bridge for the first time is to pretend that the bridge is not even there. Do nothing differently than you would if you were riding along a flat stretch of land.

If your horse becomes upset and begins to act unacceptably, do not dismount—which would reward him. Instead, move a bit further from the bridge and stand there for a few minutes. Never reward a horse for being bad. You do not want him to think that he can scare you and make you dismount. Be sure that you tell him to turn and to move away from the bridge. Never let him think that it was his idea to "flee." Move to another area and make him work, perhaps loping circles. Do not reward bad behavior by dismounting or quitting for the day, and do not get yourself hurt by forcing the issue. Tomorrow is another day. Show your horse that his obstinance only causes him to work harder. He must choose the lessor of the two evils: work hard under saddle or take a leisurely walk over the bridge. Time and patience will cure most problems, as long as the horse does not learn that he can scare you by acting badly. Always think about how the horse might interpret your actions.

Finally, the day comes to fully cross the bridge. Plan enough time to work with your horse until he will put one foot on the board. Keep his head pointed straight ahead and keep encouraging him. Sit quietly when he

Be sure to maintain a straight line when you cross, as shown here.

will stand facing the board. Turning and looking in the other direction is not an option. He must face the board. He may be five to ten feet away from it, but he must stand facing the board. Ease him forward step by step until finally he puts one foot on the board. The next time, ask for two steps, and so on. If he will cross the corner of the board, he has crossed the bridge. Be happy with that much for today. Ask for a little more each day, and remember not to let his prior actions cause you to tense your body. While you must prepare for whatever he does, you don't want to tell him to be "bad." Never start an obstacle when you are rushed for time or you may have to quit at a point that is not in the horse's best interest.

Training requires huge amounts of patience. The most important lesson is teaching a horse that he must go forward on command. If a horse has learned that he doesn't have to obey your commands to go forward at all times, work on that and then come back to the bridge. Ask him to cross first one pole on the ground, then two poles, and so on. Ask him to step on your trailer mat, on concrete (slowly, as it can be slippery), or on any type of footing that is different. Enforce going forward over small obstacles and gradually make them bigger and more difficult. Not only must your horse go forward on your command, he must go where you direct him. In most cases, a horse that is respectful of your lead line cues on the ground will also be respectful of your cues from his back. You must enforce respect at all times!

HANDLING REFUSALS

If your horse still shows major resistance to crossing the bridge, try following another horse across it. Or, put the bridge next to a wall so the wall blocks one side of the bridge and

*If a horse is afraid
of crossing the
bridge, just work
calmly around it.*

see if you can lead the horse over it. Sometimes, putting a little grain on the bridge will get the horse closer. After a few days, he should be familiar with the bridge and cross it willingly, first while being led from the ground, and then with you mounted.

Another option is to put the horse in a small pen with first one, and then as many, "bridges" as will fit in the pen. Put his food on and around them. Make him move across these sheets of plywood in some manner. Be sure that your horse cannot get hurt or injure you when you first put him into this pen. Let him learn on his own time that a sheet of plywood will not harm him.

If your horse refuses the bridge and begins to rear or spin, and you fear for your safety, it is time to enlist the aid of a professional trainer. Most horses can be taught to cross a bridge by using a step by step approach, but a few cannot. Never sacrifice your own or your horse's safety.

PAST THE PLYWOOD STAGE

As your horse becomes comfortable with walking over a sheet of plywood, ask him to stop halfway across it and stop for a few minutes. Remember that your trail horse must learn to move step by step through an obstacle. At a show you will ask him to step slowly across the bridge, and this slow and easy, step-by-step method will insure that he doesn't rush in a class. Always allow him the opportunity to drop his head to look where he is placing his feet.

If you lean your weight forward slightly and bring your rein hand a little closer to his ears as your horse drops his head, you will insure that he has freedom to lower his head and look at the bridge. This is one of the few times that looking down is acceptable. The shift in your body position will encourage him to drop his head to look where he is placing his feet.

Another trick is to sprinkle small amounts of grain along the bridge to encourage him to look down at it. Don't do this every day or he will run to the bridge to look for grain. But, on occasion, if your horse becomes complacent, the grain will perk his interest. Be sure that you move your hand up his neck and cue with your body by leaning slightly forward as he lowers his head to find the grain. You want your horse to associate the shift in your weight with the fact that he is allowed to drop his head. He should look where he is putting his feet. You will be penalized for obvious cues to get him to do this, so don't push on his neck or give any other obvious cue. Simply move your hand forward and look down at the bridge, which will shift your weight. Your horse will learn this "cue" if you give it consistently. Never pull the horse's head up as he looks at the bridge, and never punish him for dropping his head to look. The goal is to have him drop his head and look at the new bridge at a show.

MOVING TO MORE DIFFICULT BRIDGES

When your horse is comfortable with a simple bridge, increase the difficulty. Use the same slow and easy method to introduce your horse to each new type of bridge. Don't rush or push him to master each one. Proceed at his speed, not yours. Change to a painted sheet of plywood. When the horse is comfortable with a white sheet of plywood, work him on a raised bridge. The suggested minimum size for a bridge is thirty-six inches wide by six feet long.

A thirty-six inch bridge is a very small area to expect a green horse to walk across. The horse will think, "Why should I walk over this bridge when solid ground is just inches away?" Granted, the horse is performing at a walk—not a canter or gallop—but introducing a horse to a wider bridge at first will make more sense to him. Save the narrow bridge for later. Eventually, though, you will need to school over a narrow bridge at home to prepare your horse for what he will find at a show. But at first, set your horse up for success by using a wider obstacle.

Once your horse masters a simple plain colored, raised bridge, school him over a colored, raised bridge. Use the same method to ask him to cross, and be sure to praise him for doing it correctly. You can add different colors to your bridge, or make different designs—anything to add variety. A large black spot in the middle of a bridge will often cause a horse to take a second look before crossing. Some won't cross at all. Practice all variations at home to make sure that your horse is not one of the "casualties."

Add variations to your bridge only after your horse has shown calm acceptance of the previous type of bridge. In addition to flat and raised bridges, you may find a bridge with a railing. While it may look tougher, in reality the rails will guide your horse easily across the center of the bridge. This is another type of obstacle that you can introduce at home to prepare your horse in case you have a bridge with a railing at a show. Not only will it help your horse—it will help you. Often a rider will become apprehensive when she sees a new or different type of obstacle in a trail course, wondering if her horse will negotiate it. The horse will feel the rider's concern, and that alone can cause a horse to refuse. So think positively! Always expect your horse to negotiate the obstacle. Most of the time, he will.

The appearance of a finished trail horse.

hurt him. Eventually he will cross whatever is put in front of him. He will learn that he must obey your cues to go forward without questions and place his feet where you tell him.

One last tip: If you approach a bridge that your horse refused before, and you haven't had time to practice it at home, be absolutely sure that you do not think (because of his past performance) that he will object to this bridge again. If you think he will not cross it, you are telegraph a message to your horse not to cross it. In more cases than not, your horse will refuse.

SOME FINAL REMINDERS

Build your horse's trust slowly and carefully. A successful trail horse is "made" through many hours of practice and correct schooling. It does not happen by chance. You must work with your horse to develop a trusting relationship. As your horse ages and matures and gains exposure to more and more varied obstacles, you will find that he takes most obstacles in stride, provided you do not "teach" him otherwise.

Always think positively. Your horse will feel your confidence and be more likely to cross whatever is in front of him.

Get professional help if the situation warrants. Some horses, through past experience, are truly frightened of bridges. Others have learned that they do not have to obey the cue to go forward. In either case, professional help with the bridge will almost certainly help with the other trail obstacles as well. Don't be embarrassed to ask for help—that is what trainers do. They've learned the hard way how to deal with the various tricky games horses play to avoid doing a certain job.

Take note of which obstacles at a show your horse does well over and what he hesitates to cross. Then go home and try to recreate what bothered him If one type of bridge, or one color, such as yellow, bothers your

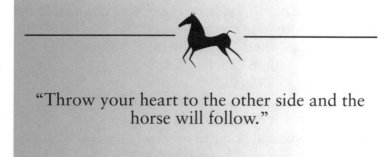

"Throw your heart to the other side and the horse will follow."

horse more than others, work with that. School over it until your horse will calmly cross whatever you put in front of him. The more you expose your horse to at home, the less apprehensive he will be when faced with new obstacles at shows. Variety at home will teach your horse that you will not put him in a situation that will

ELEVEN

TROT-OVERS
AND LOPE-OVERS

TROT-OVERS AND LOPE-OVERS are very popular in today's fast-paced trail classes. You will probably find either one or both in most classes. For that reason, be sure to school over poles at home. Don't just assume that your horse will hop over poles willing and take them in stride. While most horses can easily negotiate one log lying on the ground, jogging or loping over a series of poles in a row or in a circular or curved pattern requires lots of practice. Your horse must keep the cadence of his gait even in a given obstacle. Lengthening or shortening his stride in the middle of a jog-over or lope-over will cost points. You must practice, practice, practice if you wish to present a clean and proficient go that will gain you points for this maneuver. Allow plenty of time for your horse to learn how to perform these maneuvers with confidence and correct cadence. Train in a logical, systematic manner that allows him to develop not only the physical strength and skill, but also the mental attitude to handle such demanding maneuvers.

YOUR HORSE'S ATHLETIC ABILITY

As you begin to work over randomly spaced poles you can tell whether or not your horse has a lot of natural rate. If he trips and falls over his own feet, ask yourself if he is overweight or out of shape, in which case the suppling exercises at the beginning of this book may help him. The easiest horse to train is one that adjusts his stride naturally, with no help from his rider. He should want to avoid touching the poles and should pick up his feet and put them down carefully. You will have to work harder as a trainer if the horse doesn't show this natural ability to rate his stride.

Sometimes a horse, especially a young one, will hit one or more of the poles for days. He may need more practice to learn to watch where to put his feet, or his body may need more time to mature. However, other horses, young and old alike, will stumble over the poles time and time again, day after day. If, after a suitable amount of time, your horse continues to trip over the poles, consider giving him more time to mature before starting trail work or find a job for which he is better suited. If your goal is to have a high level trail horse, you may need to replace this horse with one more suitable. Don't think of it as a reflection of your training ability. Some horses are not naturally suited for trail, just as some people hate the

You may eventually be required to walk over elevated poles. This mare shows a finished appearance—calm acceptance, good spacing, and all on a loose rein so she can lower her head to look.

Maintaining position, feet between the poles.

Exiting—still in good form. Notice the way the blocks are used to hold the poles.

slow, controlled aspect of trail, preferring instead to ride a jumper, reiner, or barrel horse.

EQUIPMENT

I like to start with heavy poles, such as old guard rails, that will stay in place even if the horse hits them. You want him to feel if he strikes them so that he learns to place his feet more carefully in the future. An added bonus of the heavier poles is that they do not

move as easily as lighter ones. Yet, if all that you have are the standard jump poles, by all means go ahead and use them. Using the larger poles makes training a little more efficient in the beginning, but it is not an insurmountable problem if you don't have them.

After a horse learns to negotiate heavy poles, then I introduce the lighter poles. I keep some of the poles their natural color, paint others white, and still others white with stripes. If you expose your horse to variety of colors he will not be as frightened by the bright colors at a show. While many horses will take a natural colored pole or log in stride, white or striped poles might cause your horse to take a second look. He might refuse to go over the obstacle at all, run out to the side, or take a bigger stride over the first pole, causing his striding to be off for the rest of that obstacle. Use poles with different colors, for example one obstacle with all natural poles and another with striped poles. This will give him the needed confidence and experience to negotiate them correctly later in a trail class.

You can also put the ends of the poles in cement blocks to keep them in place and to help the horse to feel if he hits a pole. An added benefit is that the blocks allow you to raise the height of the poles just a few inches by using the bottom hole of the block. This helps a horse learn to pick up his feet. Learning to clear schooling poles set up this way makes poles placed flat on the ground at a show easy. This is one way that you can put the odds for success in your favor. Any time you make the schooling at home just a little harder for your horse than what he will find at a show, you prepare him for a good performance over the easier obstacles.

I suggest schooling in a snaffle bit if your horse is obedient in that type of bit. Until a horse is truly solid at these maneuvers, guiding with two hands on the reins is to your benefit. The approach to jog-overs or lope-overs may require that you do a lot of guiding initially. Riding two-handed in a snaffle makes it easy to guide a horse. Additionally, if the horse should pop over a pole or two in the beginning, you will not do as much damage to his mouth as if you caught him in the mouth with a curb bit as he jumped. However, be sure that your horse will obey your cues to stop or slow down in a snaffle. If he gets excited when first introduced to poles and lope-overs and you cannot stop him adequately in a snaffle then use your customary bit. Safety should be your first concern.

START WITH SINGLE POLES

At first, place some randomly spaced poles around your work area and walk, jog, and lope around them, allowing the horse to view these new "obstacles." Later, you can arrange your poles and boxes so you can maneuver through one obstacle and then either go to the next obstacle or

circle and take that same obstacle in a different way.

Prepare your horse for jog-overs and lope-overs (as well as for the box) by setting up single poles at randomly spaced intervals in your arena or work area. When he is warmed up and ready to pay attention to you rather than to the poles on the ground, select one pole and aim for the middle of it. Keep your horse moving at a steady cadence, and sit squarely in the saddle so you don't interfere with your horse's way of going. Try not to inadvertently cue him by wiggling or looking up, down, left or right.

Walk your horse towards the center of the pole, encouraging him forward with your legs if he feels hesitant, and allow him enough rein that if he wants to drop his head to look at the pole, he can do so. Do nothing with your body that would tell him that he should become tense or fearful. Don't tense your body in anticipation of the horse refusing or jumping the log. A log on the ground should not cause any alarm to you or your horse. Horses have been negotiating these types of obstacles for centuries. If you tense your body in any way, a horse interprets that as a sign that he should be cautious. Stay relaxed and your horse will assume that the pole is nothing to fear.

Always pick a point beyond the pole on which to focus your vision. Looking down can cause a horse to step on the pole, trip over the pole, or alter the cadence of his gait.

Direct your horse at the log and ask him to cross it. If he hesitates, use both legs to squeeze him forward. Use the reins to keep his nose pointed at the log. Be prepared for him to jump over or try to avoid the log in the initial stages of training. This introduction to poles is simply to teach your horse to lift his feet and cross each log

Begin by walking, jogging, and loping over a single pole.

in the center. He must learn to accept logs and poles as part of his life.

Incorporate poles, and later the box, into your daily schooling. Poles are always part of a trail course, whether arranged in a box, a jog-over, a lope-over, or countless other obstacles. Introduce poles to your horse slowly, then increase the degree of difficulty. Starting with a single log, rather than a series of logs, builds confidence in both you and your horse. When your horse will walk over one pole in stride without breaking rhythm, progress to a jog. When he will jog comfortably over the log, progress to a lope. Then set up three or four poles in different areas of your work area and walk over those, again from either direction.

Approach From Either Direction

Approach the poles from both directions, again until he is comfortable with jogging over a single pole. If you are using small poles and have cement blocks available, the next step would be to raise one pole and let the

horse become comfortable with a raised pole. His acceptance of one pole on the ground is the basis of this entire lesson. Time spent now getting your horse comfortable over a single pole will pay dividends later when you progress to more complicated maneuvers. Place three or four single poles around your work area and ask the horse to jog over them from both directions. Varying the pattern.

Always make a long, straight approach to each pole. Set your poles so you have room to jog to the pole, jog over the pole, and in a straight line after the pole. Later, he will need space to lope it the same way. Go over the pole and continue in a straight line. Use the long, straight line both approaching or ending the obstacle to keep your horse from cutting out to the side after exiting the poles. Choose your lines and expect the horse to follow them. Don't let him wander around looking for direction. Use your hands and legs to guide and keep him in the center of the poles.

Enforce Obedience

With this exercise you are once again enforcing total obedience. Your horse must learn to go where you tell him. Many horses have never been made to leave the comfort and security of the rail. When they are faced with straight lines and no fence to follow, or with circling, they become rattled and lose their frame or cadence. Spend the time now teaching your horse to be obedient to your every command, whether to negotiate a pole or guide in and around obstacles in the center of the arena. All of this will benefit him as he progresses in trail work.

Initially, don't ask for turns that are too tight or too sudden directly after a jog-over or lope-over. Continue for eight or ten strides after crossing

Jogging through a long line of heavy poles will help your horse learn to adjust his stride. If he bumps these heavy poles, he will soon learn to pick up his feet.

Here, he correctly places his feet centered between each pole.

the pole before you ask him to stop or turn. You can increase the degree of difficulty later.

MAINTAIN STRIDE, RHYTHM AND CADENCE

The length of a horse's stride is not only determined by prior training, but also by his conformation and size. A large horse will naturally have a longer stride, unless he has been trained to move with a shorter, more collected stride. A straight shouldered horse will naturally move with a shorter stride than will a horse with more slope to his shoulder. Don't worry if it takes longer for your horse to learn to lope through a row of poles than it does for another horse. It may be more related to his conformation or his size than his willingness to learn.

On that same note, if your horse is comfortable striding through poles three feet apart, later you can lengthen the distance to three-and-one-half or four feet so that he learns to stride out a bit. This is especially beneficial if

you show in All-Around classes or want to improve your horse's trotting stride in English or hunter classes.

USE A COMBINATION OF POLES

After your horse will calmly negotiate a single pole and walk over it, add a second pole. When he masters walking over two poles, then add three, and so on. Continue to add one pole at a time until he will walk over eight poles in sequence set twenty to twenty four inches apart. If he has to reach to meet the second pole, shorten the distance between them. If he bumps the second pole, lengthen the distance. You should use this method to find a comfortable distance to space the poles for each gait. Once your horse gains confidence and learns to stride through in rhythm, slowly inch the poles to the distance required by the rule book.

The goal is to teach your horse to carefully place his feet so that he strides through the line of poles in rhythm without touching them. You do not

Measure the distance between poles. They must be consistently spaced if you expect your horse to learn to maintain an even cadence.

INTRODUCE JOG-OVERS AND LOPE-OVERS

As you increase the degree of difficulty with the walk-over, simultaneously begin to introduce a single jog-over pole. When your horse will jog over one pole, add a second pole in line with the first one, then three, then four, and so on. Gradually work up to eight poles. Your goal at the jog is to cross poles set three feet apart, but if your horse has a long stride and cannot comfortably navigate them at three feet, then space the poles four feet apart. He should place a foot exactly in the middle of the space between poles. When he learns to go over the poles smoothly at this distance, move all the poles closer together to cause him to shorten his stride. It is important to set all the poles in a series an equal distance apart. Continue adjusting the space until you reach the required showing distance.

If you have enough poles available, set up a combination of walk-over as well as trot-over obstacles. This speeds the training process and helps to keep your horse from becoming bored. With the second set of poles, begin to increase the degree of difficulty at the walk. Set two or three poles in a straight line and walk over them. Encourage your horse to drop his head and look, and always try to keep his expression alert.

At the same time, you can introduce the single lope-over pole. Use the same method to increase the degree of difficulty at the lope by adding more lope-over poles. Remember that lope-overs require more room than the trot-overs. Space lope-overs poles seven to eight feet or more at first. Make it easy for your horse to place his feet between the poles without hitting them. Gradually work down to six or seven feet apart as is required by the rule book.

want him to rush as he exits the poles or "die" halfway through them and break gait. He should enter and exit at the same cadence. Always cross the middle of the poles when they are set in a straight line. Do not veer left or right. You will lose points in a trail class for not staying exactly centered. With a curved line of poles, cross where the distance best matches your horse's stride. Throughout this exercise you should have complete control of your horse and he should accept your cues willingly, with no sign of resentment.

REQUIRED DISTANCE BETWEEN POLES

∩ **Walkovers:** 20 to 24 inches apart for each stride

∩ **Jog-overs:** 3 to 3 1/2 feet apart for each stride

∩ **Lope-overs:** 6 to 7 feet apart for each stride.

When training walkovers, start with a comfortable distance for your horse and then gradually adjust the spacing to the required distance.

At first your horse may try to take really long strides or leap over the poles, but if you've schooled trot-overs correctly, it should not take long for him to become relaxed doing lope-overs. (An added bonus to doing the lope-over is that it is the same approach used to introduce jumps).

Space lope-over poles seven to eight feet apart and work your way down to the six or seven feet required by the rules.

BE CREATIVE WITH POLES

A minimum of fifteen or twenty poles will allow you to create various obstacles. Leave a box set up in one area and also keep a few single poles set up. Use them as a warm-up for jog-overs or lope-overs, or for jogging to a pole and stopping.

A single pole can also be side-passed. Elevate it to twelve inches. Poles arranged in the shape of a "W" can be sidepassed over or jogged through. The variety is endless. The more poles you have at your disposal, the more creative you can be, and the more time you can spend riding and schooling instead of resetting poles.

You can add variety by putting four or more poles in a slightly curved line. Your horse must stay between the bridle with the correct arc in his body to match the arc of the poles. Always cross the center of the poles, unless one side is closer together than the other side of the poles, as in a curved line. In this case, enter at a spot where the spacing matches your horse's stride. Put your horse where he can best show his ability. For example, if he hasn't yet mastered striding comfortably through poles set at three feet, jog closer to three-and-one-half feet. While a knowledgeable judge may realize that your horse is striding long,

Your horse should be relaxed as he does lope-overs.

he may appreciate the fact that you set your horse up for success. It is better to have a clean trip than it is to knock the poles because you put your horse at the wrong distance. Look for the little things that will let your horse shine. Trail is all about control—putting the horse exactly where you can ride the best.

For more variety with jog-overs and lope-overs, you can make a six, nine, or a twelve-foot box (always use multiples of three feet, depending on the gait you choose). Jog or lope into the box and on through it.

You can make a "W" or an "M" out of poles and jog across the part that matches the length of your horse's stride. Or, set up a course of poles, alternating their direction horizontally and vertically. This will require you to cross straight over the middle of one pole and then turn left (or right) to cross the center of the second pole. You can add poles as you like. When you get to the end, reverse and ride back over them. This maneuver requires your horse to steer easily. Start with the poles far enough apart that your horse has room to cross the pole and go straight

1. *Entering jog-over poles set on a curved line. Notice I've applied leg pressure to encourage her to jog over the poles.*

2. *Here, the mare is not stepping exactly in the center of the poles, but she is not bumping them.*

3. *As she exits, the mare maintains a good attitude—ears up, rein loose.*

4. *She continues nicely following the bend or arc of the poles.*

for four to eight strides before making a turn to the second pole. Shorten the distances between poles when he masters the easy method. This exercise will sharpen your horse's maneuverability and willingness to be guided as well as his footwork over poles.

Yet another obstacle that you can make is an elongated figure eight. Jog over a line of poles. At the end of the poles, continue straight until your horse feels balanced and settled, then reverse direction and re-enter from the same direction as you ended. Shorten the distance on your turns when the horse feels able to handle it.

LEARN WAGON WHEEL AND "T" LOPE-OVERS

Some of the more difficult lope-overs at a show are the wagon wheel lope-over and T-shaped lope-over. The wagon wheel requires you to lope around a circle of four poles laid on the ground, with your horse taking two strides between each pole or "spoke." This obstacle usually has a visual centerpiece, such as a flower pot. The secret to completing this obstacle? Do not look at the center. Doing so will cause your horse to veer to the inside. Remember, your horse will go where you look. Looking to the inside will make your horse move to the center and shorten his stride. If you continue looking inward, he might make one full stride, followed by a short stride before crossing a pole. Then he might get only one long stride before meeting the next pole.

Look to the next pole. Once your horse clears the first pole, your job for that pole is done. Concentrate on the next one. When he completes the stride over that pole, use your reins, seat and leg cues to set your horse up to make the slight turn to meet the next pole. Allow him to straighten his body just before he reaches the pole. Lope straight over it, and continue in this manner until you finish the wheel.

The tricky part of this maneuver is guiding your horse to the correct part of the poles so that he can make two strides between each pole. Before you take your horse though this obstacle, first walk or measure the distance between the poles. If the poles are striped red and white, you observe that to get two six-foot strides, for example, you must meet each pole at the beginning of the red stripe. If the poles are not striped, you have to visualize where to meet each pole so that it will allow your horse to make the correct number of strides. And, you need to ride the course without looking down at the poles. Find the poles in your peripheral vision, or just drop your eyes, not your entire head, to look.

To begin the wagon wheel lope-over, pick up a steady, consistently-paced lope around the arena. Wait until the horse has a consistent rhythm to his stride and can maintain that cadence. Then head toward the first spoke of the wheel. Lope over it with your horse's body in a straight line. Make a slight turn to meet the next spoke by "riding the entire horse." Use all of the aids. Don't just steer

Poles arranged in a wagon wheel pattern.

with your reins. Squeeze slightly with your legs to ask him to collect so he can use his body to make the circle. If you feel him veering to the inside, apply slightly stronger inside leg pressure to keep him out. If he begins to swing wide, apply outside leg pressure to hold him in the pattern. If he is not arcing his body between poles, use your inside leg at the girth and your outside leg slightly behind the girth as you turn. Allow him to straighten just before he comes to the next pole.

In the initial training, your horse might only be able to lope over two spokes correctly before swinging wide and missing the third. Remember, this is a difficult obstacle. Your horse must not only lope over a pole while maintaining the cadence of his gait to meet the next pole correctly, and he must be agile enough to lope a small circle. Steady his lope as you go around the arena. Then enter the obstacle again and try for three poles. Don't keep loping and loping until the horse is grasping for breath. Intersperse this training with quiet walks to keep the horse from getting rattled. When you feel a slight improvement, quit for the day. You will NOT master this obstacle in a day. Continue practicing until you can lope the entire wheel in cadence, meeting the poles in stride.

This horse is correctly completing a line of jog-over poles.

At most shows you are allowed to walk the course prior to entering. Take full advantage of this opportunity and find the distances and approaches that will show your horse to his best advantage

Another difficult obstacle requires that your horse lope straight over a pole in a horizontal position like the top of a capital "T." Continue loping parallel to the vertical pole of the "T" until you reach the bottom. Turn almost in place around the bottom of the "T." Travel parallel with the vertical pole until you reach the horizontal pole at the top once again. Cross that pole, meeting it in stride.

You can trot this pattern until your horse has some understanding of what is expected. Be sure to squeeze him around and through the corner utilizing the methods explained in the chapters on circling and serpentining. This tight corner is the most difficult aspect of the "T," but a horse with good natural rate will meet the top pole in stride. Progress to loping the "T" after your horse has mastered it at a trot.

Practice wrapping your horse around your inside leg and squeezing him through the turn at the bottom of the "T." Make the tight turn and continue to lope. Begin with a wider, easier turn and slowly, over a period of weeks, teach your horse to make a tight turn.

Tight turns teach your horse to guide easily, and to collect and use his hind end on the turn. If you utilized the suppling maneuvers in the first chapters, this will be easier for your horse.

DO NOT PUSH YOUR HORSE

Introduce these difficult obstacles slowly to your junior horse so that he will be prepared to face them, if not now, then certainly later as a senior trail horse. Never push for more than he can give. Continue to lope over poles set in various configurations. With time, he'll handle the more difficult obstacles with ease. Adding speed to a maneuver increases the degree of difficulty. Lope overs and tight turns made at the jog or lope are some of the hardest maneuvers for a horse to perform. Practice at home, but never school your horse into the ground. Take the time for a quiet, relaxing walk to let him mentally absorb what you are asking of him. Don't drill your horse. When he gets a slight understanding of a tough obstacle, let him rest and relax. Follow with an easy obstacle.

Your horse will need a complete break from time to time when you are working on the tougher obstacles. Don't sour him by asking him to perform beyond his ability. It takes time to learn to handle these tough obstacles. Continue to work on getting control of your horse's head, hips, and shoulders. Soon, you will be able to maneuver through any type of obstacle, turn, or pattern at a show.

TWELVE

THE BOX

THE BOX is a common obstacle in trail patterns. It is fashioned out of equal length poles, rails or logs positioned in a square. What you do in the box is designated by the pattern. You may be required to enter the box and execute a 360- or 180-degree turn. You could be asked to stop before the box, walk into the box and make a 180-degree turn to reverse your direction and then exit the box. Or you might be asked to jog or lope through the box, or across the corner of the box. There are numerous possible variations of the

above. For example, the pattern could call for you to jog into the box, stop, and make a 360-degree turn without touching the poles, then step out of the box facing the same direction as you entered.

Boxes that are set up for a turn are five feet square. For lope-overs, the box must be six or seven feet square so that your horse can stride comfortably over the poles. For jog-overs, the poles of the box must be between three feet and three feet, six inches. The size of the box can be can be doubled or tripled to

Enter the box and perform a 360-degree turn.

Entering the box in dead center makes the obstacle difficult. Start closer to either the left or right side to help your horse turn without bumping a pole.

position the poles the correct distance for striding over them. As an example, poles set six feet apart double the three feet required in the rule book for a jog-over. This gives your horse space to take a second stride before jogging over the next pole.

Some patterns ask you to jog over a corner of the box. To execute these properly, measure three-foot sections for a jog-over and seven-foot sections for a lope-over (or double or triple those distances) so you can position your horse accordingly. Make it easy for him to stride through without touching the poles.

TURNING IN THE BOX

When your horse has learned to walk, jog, and lope over poles without becoming nervous in any way, begin to

introduce various maneuvers such as the box. Initially, set the poles of your box anywhere from eight to ten feet square. Starting with a large box introduces it in a non-threatening manner. Walk your horse into the box and stop. Let him stand for a minute to keep him from anticipating. When he settles, use the same method as you used to make the corner of the "L" back-up— ask him to rotate around your leg. It should feel like he has a pole in his middle like a merry-go-round horse and is rotating around it. Do not let him pivot like a reining horse (with his body aligned from head to tail and a hind foot planted). There is not enough room in the small box to turn in this way.

Use your right neck-rein cue to guide the horse's head to the left and your left leg to push his rear to the right. Pay attention to where he places his feet. Ask him to take one step so he faces the first diagonal corner of the box. Let him settle and relax. When he feels comfortable in that position, ask him to step again until he faces the next diagonal corner. Let him settle and relax. Ask for another step and continue until you have completed a 360-degree turn. Stop. Wait. Then step out of the box.

Never allow your horse to walk out of the box until you cue him to do so. If your horse gets too close to the logs during training, back him a step or two away from them. Make one 360-degree turn in place and stop. After exiting the box, don't rush to perform another obstacle. Walk around your work area to give the horse time to absorb what he just did and what cues you used to tell him. This really helps to keep a horse quiet. In addition, he will learn the maneuver in a shorter period of time than if you repeated it over and over. Keep it quiet and simple. Let the horse step out of the box on a relaxed rein. He

1. You may be asked to jog through the box.

2. To teach the turn in the box, enter the box and stop.

3. Take a step, rotating around the horse's middle (like a merry-go-round pole) to the first corner.

4. Go to the second corner. When turning left, use a left neck rein to move the horse's front and left leg pressure to move the hip right. Continue until you make a 360-degree turn and exit the box where you entered. Be careful not to bump the poles.

will learn to perform in the same manner the next time. Relaxing and giving him time to absorb the new information sets it in his mind. If you rush to work on a maneuver again, a horse seems to assume that he is being corrected for doing something wrong.

GO SLOWLY!

Many riders don't realize the importance of going slowly, especially when training a young horse. They rush a horse through his training or though the obstacles because they are in a hurry to finish the chores, go to work, feed the kids, and bale the hay. Just imagine that you were back in first grade and your teacher yelled, "All right, kids. Quick! Say your ABC's. . . That wasn't good enough, say them again. Quick! Hurry! All right, now count to twenty. Quick! Hurry! Do it again, you missed fifteen. Count again. Good. Now what is one times one? Two times two? Four times four? What do you mean I'm going too fast?"

One way to cure rider anticipation is to wear a set of head phones and walk your horse for the length of a song. If you have a horse that has a lot of forward motion, stop the horse and make him stand for the length of a song. Patience is a virtue when training. Be sure that the music you listen to is quiet and mellow, not aerobic training songs! You not only want to teach your horse to move slowly; you want to teach yourself to slow down and enjoy the music.

On that same note, never perform a series of obstacles one right after another, such as a 360-degree turn in the box followed by jogging through the box and then sidepassing half of the box. In the horse's mind, these three separate obstacles become one large obstacle. He will try to do all three obstacles in a row rather than wait for you to tell him how to proceed. Horses learn by repetition. Always think about what you are doing so you can use that concept to your benefit.

When the horse understands the concept of turning inside the box, you can shorten the size of your box. The smallest box allowed is five feet, so be sure that your horse can turn in place in a five-foot square area. Expect this to take one to three months, depending on your horse.

Always ask your horse to move step by step. If the pattern calls for a 180-degree turn, he must rotate halfway and exit the box facing in the opposite direction. If he over-turns and tries to do a 360-degree because that is all that you have taught him, he will not exit the box in line with the next obstacle. Therefore, always make your horse turn step by step and obey your cues for when to go and when to stop. He must not anticipate. Remember, it is not the speed in which you turn but the precision and correctness of your form that is being judged.

When your horse can turn 180 degrees without touching the logs, ask him to complete the 360-degree turn slowly in one fluid motion. Use your legs and cue him to move a bit quicker. You will need the "move quicker" cue at shows, so make it consistent. Do not cue him to go quicker every time you do a 360-degree turn. Vary the speed. If he begins to rush, and especially if he begins to hit the poles, slow down immediately and return to the step, wait, step, wait routine.

Now, begin to vary the pattern by making a quarter turn, stopping, standing for three to four minutes, and then exiting the box. To really change the horse's mind, turn three or four steps in one direction, hesitate, and then turn three or four steps in the other direction. Be sure that you practice turning both left and right. You never know which a pattern will require.

In addition to the turn-in-place in the box, some patterns will ask you to stop before the box and then walk in. Others will require you to trot into the box and then stop. Practice all options so that you are prepared no matter what the pattern requires. Learn how far before the box you need to cue your horse to stop, so you will automatically do this at a show. And don't stop your horse at the box every time you practice. Occasionally, walk toward a pole and stop before you reach it. Other times, jog to the same or a different pole and ask for a stop there. Always vary workouts in order to keep your horse alert and listening to you.

You must learn to tell when your horse has exited the box at a walk, jog, or lope with all four feet, and when to begin to cue him to proceed to the next obstacle. You should feel when his hind feet exit the box by the way he steps. If this is difficult for you, ask a helper on the ground to work with you until you learn it. Teach your horse to depart promptly when you cue for a new gait. Practice this with or without a box. You can use a single pole or the open arena. Never cue your horse to move off at a new gait if his hind feet are still in the box. He might trip or stumble, losing points in a class.

Observe where you will finish the turn in the box so that you are set up facing in the correct line of travel for the next obstacle. These minor mistakes, which are often overlooked, can separate the first place from the sixth place horse. Attention to detail is critical.

JOG AND LOPE THE BOX

Your horse must also learn both to jog and lope through the box. Start with the box set to a size that your horse can comfortably stride through and work your way down to the seven-foot box that the rules require. If your horse is comfortable loping over a single pole in practice, start with a box seven to eight feet square, depending on the length of his stride, and lope through it. As you gain more control of your horse, shorten the radius of the box to seven feet. Make it easy in the initial stages and then tighten the distance. Don't scare or over-face your horse while he is learning these maneuvers. Give him plenty of time to master the basic maneuver, and only then increase the degree of difficulty.

Jog into the box and straight out of it. Next, vary the pattern by stopping in front of the box from a jog. Another time walk into the box, turn, and exit. Lope through the box. Teach your horse that he must wait for and obey your cue for whichever option you will ask for this time. Should he stop in the box or jog through it? Lope through it, or walk into it and turn a 180- or a 360-degree turn? Don't punish him for performing the "wrong" option. He is trying to do what he thinks is correct. You must learn to feel

You may be asked to jog to the box.

Some patterns ask that you lope through the box.

what your horse is thinking and then use your hands and legs to show him what you want. Correct him and consider whether or not you have inadvertently taught him to follow a set pattern rather than obey your cues.

ELEVATE THE BOX

Once you have mastered the basic box maneuvers, repeat the entire sequence, elevating the poles three or four inches. The maximum allowable height to the top of the poles at a show is twelve inches for walk-overs, eight

You may be required to sidepass all or part of a box.

At the corner, use the same method as when sidepassing the "W." Steady the horse's head. Maintain enough pressure that she doesn't walk forward but not so much that she backs out. Hold your left leg slightly off her side and use a right leg cue behind the girth to push her hips around the corner.

Straighten and sidepass the next pole.

options you practice, the less the horse will be intimidated by at a show. If you want to become competitive, your horse must maintain the cadence of his gait no matter what the obstacle.

KNOW HOW YOUR HORSE REACTS

You must know how your horse reacts to various cues so that your lines from obstacle to obstacle will be straight (unless specified otherwise), prompt, and correct. How much neck rein (or direct rein) is required to turn your horse? How much leg pressure is required to move his hip left or right? How much pressure is required for him to depart into each gait or to stop him?

If you wear spurs at home, wear the same type to a show. If you don't wear spurs at home, the day of a show is not the time to try them. While some people use a different bit at shows, be sure that the horse accepted that type of bit prior to the day of the show. Don't spring surprises on your horse and expect him to show his best.

inches for trot-overs, and eight inches for lope-overs. (Elevated obstacles are not allowed in novice classes.) Place the poles in cement blocks or cupped or notched holders so they cannot move and trip the horse. Increase the degree of difficulty slowly, in stages, and only after your horse is comfortable at the previous level.

Assuming that you followed the earlier methods and squeezed your horse through the circles and serpentines, using your legs to push him forward through the raised poles should be a familiar cue. Soon, an elevated box will be no more difficult for him than the basic box, and the elevated jog-over no harder than the basic one. The more

THIRTEEN

THE SLICKER, MAIL BOX, AND OPTIONAL OBSTACLES

THE LIST of optional obstacles that can be used in a trail class includes putting on and removing a slicker, removing and replacing articles from a mail box, and carrying an object from one part of the arena to another. The only stipulation is that the article to be carried must be an object that could reasonably be carried on a trail ride. A horse that is not easily ruffled by various obstacles, that listens obediently to his rider's cues to help him maneuver through a difficult obstacle, and that picks his way through an obstacle when the situation warrants it, will score highest in a trail class. In fact, these qualities are appreciated in trail horses both in and out of the arena.

Show committees are getting more and more enterprising in their design of trail classes, and as you advance from the junior to senior (horses five and over), the obstacles get tougher and tougher. For those reasons alone, it is wise to select a horse that "has a head on his shoulders"—one that doesn't get rattled easily and that willingly obeys the cues of his rider.

READ YOUR HORSE

Many of today's show horses have been handled from birth and are bred to be calm and accepting of the many things that we humans ask of them. For those horses, picking up a slicker and laying it over their shoulders will present little, if any, problem. Nevertheless, before expecting your horse to accept a bright yellow plastic slicker that may crackle or blow in the wind, spend time working with him on the ground. Let him become accustomed to such a sight. The best time to introduce a new object is at the end of a work session. The horse will not have an abundance of excess energy to give him an excuse to buck or spook when faced with a slicker the first few times. Always set yourself up for success. Introduce new objects when your horse is tired.

Learn to read your horse. If he fears every new thing until it is introduced over and over in a calm and non-threatening manner, then keep using that approach. If your horse easily accepts new objects, then you can proceed a little quicker. A few days spent

Different associations use different obstacles in trail classes. For example, the Paint Horse Association may ask for a jump while the American Quarter Horse Association will not. Read your rulebook to see what your association requires as mandatory obstacles.

START WITH A SIMPLE OBJECT

Rather than start with a bright yellow slicker, introduce your horse to a smaller object first. A towel or saddle blanket works well. I often use a white bath towel because it is light weight and easy to carry. To begin, approach your horse from the ground. This is for your safety as well as for his. While holding your horse, walk up to him and let him sniff or look at the towel or blanket. If he begins snorting and backing away, you need to move slowly. Don't rush up to him. Try not to let your body language suggest apprehension. Be confident, steady, and slow.

Once your horse has looked over the towel, or whatever you chose to introduce to him, begin rubbing it on his neck. Talk to him in a soothing voice if he seems worried. Tell him that he is behaving as he should. If a horse seems slightly nervous, I will rub him for a few seconds with the towel. Then I lay it over my arm (or nearby on a stool) as I rub his neck and tell him what a good boy he is. When he relaxes and settles, I repeat the procedure several times. Often you will hear the horse sigh in relief, as if he's saying, "Whew. Got through that. I guess it really wasn't so bad after all."

Continue to rub the towel over his neck and praise him as needed until he accepts it. Let the horse tell you how much he can accept at any one given time. If he is very spooky, you can quit for the day when he accepts it on his neck and repeat the procedure the following day. It shouldn't take nearly as long on the following day, and you can advance further. If the horse readily accepted the towel on his neck, let it lay across and rub it

quietly in the initial training can save you time down the trail. Your horse must learn to trust that you will not put him in a situation that will hurt him. This will not only overcome his apprehension of the current object, but will leave him with good feelings about the next new object. Take your time.

You can familiarize your horse to many of the objects commonly found in a trail class. However, there is a pretty good chance that one day your horse will be faced with something that he has never seen. Rather than trying to teach your horse to accept one object, such as the slicker, try to teach him to accept all objects that you might carry on him. Although it may take a little more time in the beginning, it is sure to pay off later.

back and forth. Then lay it over his withers and rub it back and forth over his back. When he will stand for that, rub it over his hind quarters and then let it drape over his tail. If at any time your horse begins to move as if he is frightened, move the towel back to a place where he previously accepted it. Look for a few brief seconds when he seems to accept the towel and then remove it and rub or scratch his neck until his head drops and he seems settled. Repeat the procedure. Stop any time that the horse shows a few seconds of acceptance.

This is the same method that I use to teach a horse to accept fly spray or any type of spray. Give one or two squirts, put the bottle down and rub the horse's neck until he settles. When his head drops, squirt his neck once or twice more and then rub it. Some horses will accept the spray by the end of the first day. Others need three or four days. Take your time when introducing any thing new. Introduce it briefly and take it away. Let the horse think about it for a moment and allow him to settle. Repeat until he accepts the new object with ease. Teaching him to accept one object will help him accept that you will not hurt him, yet tell him that you do expect him to stand and obey your request.

BODY LANGUAGE

Horses read your body language more than you can even imagine. I found this out the hard way quite a few years ago. The first colt I tried to clip was a terror. He didn't want to be in the same barn as those clippers, never mind have them touch his face or bridle path. The next colt to be trimmed was not nearly as bad, yet when he began to fret, I immediately thought, "Oh no. Here we go again." I began to dread the initial clipping experience. A few babies later, I asked a friend to hold the colt while I went to get something. I came back and she was clipping this colt as if he'd done it his whole life, which, I'll admit, wasn't very long at that point. Yet he had never been clipped before. The moral? Because she assumed that I had clipped this baby before, she approached him with the attitude "This is just one more thing that we silly humans do. I know you have done this before." The colt took it in stride. The next colt I clipped, I made myself act the same way. He stood and let me clip him. I tried the theory on a few more and found that my attitude made a big difference. Once I learned to use it while clipping, I begin to use the same attitude about other things. While it is certainly not fool proof, it is one more way to "set yourself up for success." Don't "tell" a horse to be afraid with your body language. Tell him, "All is well, this is no big deal and I expect you to behave and accept it."

1. If your horse objects to the slicker, you accustom him to it first from the ground. You can also start with a smaller, less noisy, item such as a towel.

2. Be sure your horse accepts the slicker before you try to pick it up while mounted.

3. Be prepared if your horse spooks or bolts when you first introduce a slicker. Don't sacrifice your safety. Your horse will learn, given enough time.

THE SLICKER

Allow plenty of time for this lesson so that you do not need to rush. Also, allow enough days in advance before he must carry a slicker or other object. Once your horse accepts a large towel, repeat the procedure with a saddle blanket or other object. When he seems to accept those objects, get the slicker and repeat the procedure. When he will let you rub the slicker all over his body, then teach him to accept it over his saddle. This shouldn't cause him any alarm.

The easiest way is to rub the slicker over his saddle at the end of your lesson. When he accepts it, quit and put him up for the day. With some horses, you can advance to this point in a day. End at that point, and wait until the following day to finish teaching about the slicker while mounted. Think slow. Take your time. That one day may be the difference between a horse that accepts the slicker and succeeding objects or one that blows up and then takes weeks to get back to this point in training.

Remember, what you teach a horse today, he learns tomorrow. Stop on a good note today and your horse should be prepared to accept more tomorrow. Give him time to think about what he did that caused him to get rewarded.

On the following day, if your horse is the type that must have his warm up or play time before getting down to business, warm him up accordingly. After he settles, hang the slicker on a pole (as you might find it in a trail class) or lay it over the arena fence. Walk past the slicker as you follow your normal schooling routine. Let the slicker be part of the surroundings. Let your horse look if he chooses. Be ready in case he spooks, but remember not to let him feel your

4. Once your horse accepts the slicker, lay it over her forehand, in front of the saddle.

5. Then place it over her back. You may also be asked to put a raincoat on and take it off.

When practicing, purposely stop six to ten feet away from the pole.

Then sidepass to it. This way, if for some reason your horse does not stop where he should, you have the tools in place to still put him into the proper position.

apprehension through your body. As he shows signs of accepting, or when he no longer tries to avoid the slicker, begin to move him closer to it as you pass by it. At the end of your lesson, walk your horse up to the slicker and stop with the slicker in line with your arm. It is a little easier and a little safer to reach forward for the slicker than to have to twist backwards in the saddle to reach it. Let your horse stop and settle. If he is a curious horse, watch that he doesn't take the slicker in his mouth and possibly pull it and the pole to the ground. That could cause him to spook and would certainly set him back. Relax and let him stand there for a minute or two. Then slowly reach for the slicker and slowly lay it over the front of your saddle. Let your horse adjust to having the slicker over the saddle. Again, you must read your horse to know how much to ask for on this first day. If he is calm and accepting, rub the slicker up and down his neck. Then hold the slicker steady and let your horse think about that. Move it around again and then hold it steady as he absorbs this new piece of equipment laying over him. Lift the slicker up and put it over your shoulder, first from the front and then over your back. Stop, relax, and let him absorb this. Hang the slicker back on the pole and slowly walk off.

On the next day, repeat these steps. If your horse has accepted them calmly, lay the slicker over the top of his rump. When he accepts that, slide it back and forth. Be sure to lay the slicker on both his left and right sides. You never know from which side of the obstacle you will be asked to approach. Prepare your horse for either side now. Leave nothing to chance. Stop on a good note. Don't overdo it on these first few days.

Teach the Horse to Stand While You Drop the Reins

On the following day, if all has/gone well and your horse easily stands without moving when you drop the reins, put the slicker on. You might be asked to do this in a class and it is best to practice at home. If your horse doesn't stand when you drop the reins, then that is something that you need to work on with your horse.

Go back to basics and reinforce the meaning of the word "Whoa!" Lift the reins to tell him to stop. Be sure that you release all rein pressure the instant that he does stop. Drop your hand to his neck to simulate standing with the reins laid on his neck. If he takes a step, immediately take a hold of his mouth (lift your reins to stop him) as you say "Whoa." Release as soon as he stops. If he takes another step, immediately make him back four to six steps, say "Whoa," and release all rein pressure. Praise your horse if stands; correct him if he doesn't. He may not learn this lesson in a day, especially if you haven't enforced that *whoa* means stop and stand. You must continue this training for as long as it takes if you plan to show in trail.

Let Your Horse Dictate the Speed of Progression

If your horse was skittish at any point with the slicker, stop at that point, let him relax so he understands that a slicker is nothing to get upset over. Then quit for the day. On the following day, add a little more, rewarding the horse for good behavior. If he wouldn't let you get close to the slicker, or if he panics once you pick it up, go back to your ground work. Rub the slicker over and around him until he accepts it. Then try again.

Some horses will accept the slicker in a few days, while others will take longer. Don't try to rush your horse. You can hang the slicker in front of his stall so that he has the opportunity to see it. Each time you go by the horse's stall, take the slicker in and lay it over his back. Move it up and down, back and forth, as he will allow. Please remember, if your horse is excessively nervous do not jeopardize your safety in any way. Start with a towel if you have to. If you can hang it over or by his feed, you can remain safely outside of the stall as your horse gains confidence. Don't enter the stall with a horse that is clearly frightened by a particular object. Hanging objects that a horse is somewhat nervous about around his stall can help him to overcome his fear on his time, with little risk to you.

Polish Your Approach

Once a horse accepts the slicker, you can begin to polish your approach to it. The pattern may ask you to put it on or just lay it over your horse. Walk your horse in a straight line (unless the pattern directs you differently) to the slicker. If your horse is not close enough to the slicker to make it easy for you to reach it without leaning out of your saddle, ask your horse to sidepass until you are in position. Practice this at home. Your horse may not want to get close to the slicker. Teach him that he must put you in position so that you don't have to lean over to get it. Leaning over not only looks bad, it is unsafe. Practice getting in the correct position both from the left and right sides, moving forward and backwards as needed, and side passing both left and right.

Make your horse stop and stand. Pick up the object. In the case of a slicker or raincoat, take it off the pole and put it on or lay it over the saddle. Some judges will ask that you only pick up the slicker and lay it over the horse, rather than putting it on all the way. This saves time in a class. If you are asked to pick the slicker up on your right side, lay it over the front of your horse and down his right side. Then drape it down his left side, swing it to the back of the horse and return it to the pole. Your goal is to show your horse's acceptance of the slicker swinging over his body. He should stand completely still.

If you know that your horse doesn't like the slicker on his rump, simply omit that from your demonstration. If he only lets you drape the slicker over his left side and not the right side, omit the right side until such a time as he has learned to accept the slicker there. Show off your horse's good points and minimize his bad. Even if every other entrant in the class swings the slicker over the horse's rump and you know that your horse doesn't like it there, don't do it. Never ask for something that you are not entirely sure that you will get. The time for chances is at home, not in the show pen. Your horse may grow to accept the slicker as he

ages or be-comes more well trained. For now, however, it's better to omit that particular part of the exercise. Show your horse to his best advantage. There's always another show, another pattern, a different judge, another day. A finished trail horse takes a long time to "make." Go home and continue to practice in a safe and controlled manner.

THE MAIL BOX

While a mail box doesn't present nearly the problems that a slicker does, your horse must still put you in the correct position to take the mail out of the box. He must stand still and allow you to reach the mail and show it to the judge. Once again, walk your horse in a straight line to the box so that he is lined up parallel with the box. Sidepass to get closer to the mail box if needed.

You should stop with the box at or slightly before your arm. If your horse tak tak takes a ste ste step too mao mao

Approach the mailbox and line up parallel to it.

Remove the mail and show it to the judge.

Replace the mail and shut the mailbox door. Your horse should stand on a loose rein.

many, backbackback him intly where you must begin to cue your horse to stop so that you know how much time he needs to obey your signal to stop.) Take the mail out of the box, lift it high enough that the judge can see it, smile, and then replace the mail. Let your horse settle briefly if needed. Be sure his head is aimed at the next obstacle before you ask your horse to move off at the designated gait.

In most cases, you will be asked to take the "mail" out of the box, show it to the judge, and then replace it. Your horse must stand on a loose rein and not try to walk off. You might have to lean down to reach the box. Be absolutely sure that you don't inadvertently bump or poke your horse with one leg or the other as you are reaching for the mail. He could mistake that for a cue to go forward or sidepass. Keep your legs still and gracefully reach for the mail. Your goal is a polished, professional appearance.

OTHER OPTIONAL OBSTACLES

Any obstacle that you might reasonably find on a trail ride can be used in a trail class. You may be asked to pick up an obstacle and show it to the judge, or to carry it from one place in the arena to another. Examples of objects normally found on a trail ride include a pair of saddle bags, a coiled lariat rope, or a nylon windbreaker in place of the yellow slicker. If you go slowly and teach your horse the basic elements with the slicker, he should perform the other obstacles with relative ease. Practicing with varied objects at home will give you more insight to your horse's weak and strong points. Try to increase his confidence in his weak areas, but remember to practice those obstacles that are his strong points on occasion to be sure they remain his strong points.

Flowers and shrubs are often used to decorate, or as part of an obstacle. Here, they mark the boundaries on an "L" back-up.

TREES, SHRUBS AND FLOWERS

Course designers use a lot of filler material, such as shrubs and flowers. Not only do these make the course more eye appealing, they are used as parts of the obstacles themselves. For example, you might be asked to serpentine around small potted shrubs. These should present few problems, but as the old saying goes, "Don't (let your horse) eat the daisies!" Teach your horse from the first day you ride him that eating while he has a bit in his mouth and a saddle on his back is not acceptable. Riding a horse that refuses to perform a certain obstacle is not nearly as embarrassing as riding a horse that tries to grab a bite of the greenery from a potted plant! Imagine your horse exiting the latest trail class with a daisy protruding from his mouth. While it might make for points with the spectators, it will not gain points from the judge.

FOURTEEN

THE WATER
OBSTACLE

A WATER OBSTACLE can be included in the optional trail obstacles in shows, particularly AQHA trail classes. There may be a water box. Metal or slick-bottom boxes are not allowed.

If your horse ran in a pasture that included a pond or a stream, a water obstacle should present few problems. If he grew up in a stall or a dry paddock, it may take a little longer to teach him not to fear water.

If you have progressed through the training as outlined in this book, you should have control over your horse's head, hips, and shoulders. That will make training your horse to cross water relatively easy, even if he shows a preference for avoiding it the first time. He knows that he must obey your cues to go forward without question, and go where you direct. A water obstacle is one more test of your horse's willingness to go forward on command in the direction that you choose.

MAKE IT INVITING

If you have a small stream or shallow pond, you can train your horse to cross water there. If you don't, then you will have to make your own water obstacle (puddle). Find a low spot that holds water when it rains. Use that following a rain storm, or fill it with a hose. If you can't find a spot in an area where you can work your horse, make a puddle. Use a shovel to take dirt out of the center and toss it to the edges to create a bank. Make your pool long enough (ten to twelve feet) so that the horse cannot just step to the side to avoid the water. Make it wide enough front to back (eight to ten feet) that he doesn't try to pop over the puddle to avoid getting his feet wet, rather than walking sedately across as he must do in trail. Any intelligent horse left to his own devices will probably avoid water if the puddle is too small. He is not intentionally trying to make you mad by refusing to put his feet in the water. Later, after the horse thoroughly understands what you expect, you can use a smaller water obstacle. Using one that is too small in the beginning stages will teach a horse ways to avoid water, rather than to cross it step by step correctly as he must in a class.

Don't lose your temper if your horse does try to jump the water. He must learn that not only do you want him to cross the water, but you want him to cross in a manner that is acceptable to you. If you get angry, the horse could interpret the water obstacle as a

Let your horse look at the water, but not drink it, at least when showing.

You can make a puddle to teach your horse to cross smoothly and willingly. This mare is an old pro at water crossing.

place to avoid! That is another reason why you need to use a training obstacle that naturally encourages the horse to do what you want.

INTRODUCE THE OBSTACLE

Walk your horse towards the middle of the obstacle. Not only is this the correct way to approach in a class, it also encourages the horse to cross the water. If he is closer to one edge or the other, he might choose the easy way and step around the obstacle, rather than go through it. Positioning your horse in the center discourages that type of thinking. Teach him to cross in a straight line. Keep his head between the bridle, using your reins to guide his head straight across the obstacle and your legs and seat to send him forward over it. If he tries to turn left, correct him with a right direct rein, and vice versa.

If your horse hesitates when approaching the obstacle, squeeze him forward with both legs to send him into and across the water. If he begins to back up, rear, or use other evasive tactics, ask him to go as close to the water as he will comfortably go. Let him stand and settle. Then ask for one more step forward. Reward him for that one step by letting him rest, relax and absorb what he just did to be allowed to rest. Continue in this manner until you reach the other side. If he crossed the water easily, walk back across the water using the same steps that caused him to cross the first time. Then take a relaxing walk and quit for the day.

If you choose to introduce water on an actual trail, the best way is to accompany a friend on a quiet, well-mannered horse that will cross water easily. Follow the lead horse back and forth across the water several times the first few days. Eventually, you lead while the other horse follows. Don't make it be big deal. Follow the other horse across the stream, then turn and lead the way back with your horse.

The problem with streams or pools of water is that some horses try to paw the water or stop and lie down in it. Use enough pressure to keep your horse moving forward until he is completely through the obstacle.

DON'T TENSE YOUR BODY

No matter how you choose to teach the water obstacle to your horse, remember—do not tense your body in anticipation of the horse spooking or refusing the obstacle. If you tense up, you are saying to your horse, "I don't think that either of us should get too close to that water. What do you think?"

Because you are the boss of this horse and rider relationship, your horse will reply (with his actions), "Sure thing, boss! If you aren't sure, then I'm not sure either. Hang on! I'll get us out of here," as he rolls back and leaves you sitting in the dust.

The only secret to "making" a horse cross water is to insist that he always obey your cues to go forward and goes where you direct. This begins long before training for the water obstacle. If he'll put one foot in the water on one day, he'll put two feet in the next day.

To put the situation in your favor, walk to the water crossing as if you were riding a clear spot on the trail. Don't even think about the water. Look to the other side as if you were already there. Do not change the way you ride. Don't clamp your legs around your horse's middle or stiffen your body, anticipating a spook. Tell the horse that he must cross the water

Don't forget to enjoy your horse and the skills you learn for trail class!

by sitting deeply in the saddle (without tensing) and squeezing your legs just as if you were asking him to walk into a box that he has done a thousand times before. Work on crossing water two or three times a week for a couple of weeks, or until your horse accepts water as just one more obstacle.

Finally, try to recreate a show ring water hazard to prepare him for what he will find in a trail class. Build a wooden box with six-inch high sides and line it with heavy plastic. Put a few inches of water in it and ask your horse to cross. Use the same method that caused him to cross the water earlier and send him through this new obstacle. Go through that obstacle until he seems comfortable and unruffled. Then relax, knowing that you have done your homework.

THE WATER-SHY HORSE

There are a few horses that may present a more serious problem when faced with water the first time, whether because of past training or the horse's view of water. With this type of horse, find a small paddock where you can create a puddle for him to cross. Put his hay on one side, and grain on the other. Encourage him to think of being around water as a nice place. When he settles in the small paddock and will walk across on his own, try to ride him across the same puddle. Be very insistent. Do not let the horse feel he has the option of saying "No!" Sit on his back with his nose pointed at the water. Wait until he has calmed down, then ask him to take a step forward. Let him settle once more and then ask for another step. Continue until you reach the other side.

At the very minimum, try to get the horse close to the water or to put a foot in the water. Ask him to hold that position until you ask him to move. Then, ask him to go forward to that spot once more, relax, and then ask him to move further. Continue in this manner and eventually, even if takes one week or three weeks, your horse should learn to negotiate the water obstacle with ease. Always enforce forward motion every time you ask for it.

It may seem as if it takes forever to get this horse to cross a water obstacle when you ask. However, in most cases, once the horse learns to cross, that training will stay with him for life. You must be assertive enough to tell the horse that refusing is not an option, yet patient enough to proceed one step at a time when necessary.

FIFTEEN

THE SHOW: PUTTING IT ALL TOGETHER

As TRAIL GAINS in popularity, the obstacles become more difficult and varied, with more emphasis placed on the horse's manner and way of going. High points go to the horse that negotiates the obstacles with style and some degree of speed. The horse must accept the rider's cues to get through an obstacle correctly, show no sign of resentment, and be capable of picking his way through an obstacle if the situation warrants.

A trail horse is not required to work on the rail. The three gaits—walk, jog, and lope—must be included in the pattern. A minimum of thirty feet is required for a horse to jog and at least fifty feet must be included in the pattern to show a horse's lope. The judge evaluates these gaits and scores them in the pattern. The tight distances for the jog and lope require your horse to depart fluidly and promptly. Being in the wrong gait or on the wrong lead is penalized. A flying lead change is optional, not mandatory, and is scored under gaits or way of going.

Junior horses (five years and younger) may be shown in a snaffle bit or bosal (hackamore). A mechanical hackamore with shanks is not allowed. When riding a junior horse in a snaffle, you are to cross the reins over the horse's neck and hold them in both hands. You must ride a horse six or over one-handed in a shank bit. Reins cannot be switched from hand to hand, except to change while working an obstacle such as a gate. In addition, the rider's hands must remain clear of the horse and saddle. Always check your rule book for bits that are allowed and those that are illegal.

You don't want to make a clean trip, only to find out that your bit is not allowed.

PLAN YOUR APPROACH

Patterns are posted an hour or so before class. Read the pattern carefully and plan your approach to and path between obstacles so your horse can negotiate the pattern to the best of his ability. A horse that follows and executes the pattern exactly as written will always score over a horse that deviates from the pattern in some way. A horse that completes each obstacle in the pattern cleanly must score over a horse that has a major fault such as refusing an obstacle or knocking part of an obstacle down. Slow and correct is the way to go. Only when your horse has consistently demonstrated his ability over

The show secretary may be able to answer your questions about the course. Don't be afraid to ask, especially when you are first starting. Horse people are the best people around and most will help if they can.

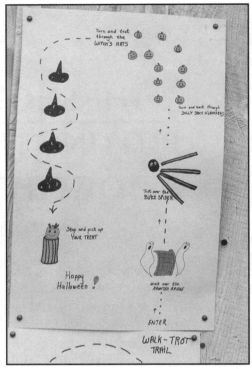

Your trail pattern should be posted at least an hour prior to your class. Study it carefully.

obstacles should you begin to ask for a little more speed, and then only on the obstacles that you know your horse performs well.

If your horse does not yet guide fluidly in reverse, back one step at a time in the back-up obstacle. It is better to go slowly and correctly, staying within the guide poles, rather than rush and bump a pole or step outside the guides. The same is true when working the gate. If your horse is not yet ready to maneuver smoothly around the gate, hesitate briefly to let him settle before he becomes flustered. Trail is not a timed event. Points are awarded for the maneuvering correctly through each obstacle. Let your horse become comfortable with working different obstacles. The speed will come later.

Carefully observe the diagram. It should give you a clue as to how to best negotiate this particular course.

Look at the entrance to each obstacle. Does the pattern have a wide circle leading to an obstacle? Do you enter at an angle or straight? Those may be the keys to riding the obstacle cleanly. Look at the course after the obstacles have been set up. Does what you planned from reading the pattern match what you see on the ground in front of you? Whenever possible, walk the pattern. Find the best route for your horse. If your horse does better with a particular obstacle when he has a long straight approach, then look to see if you can ride the obstacle—using the pattern as written—with a long straight approach. Can you gain a few feet by cornering wider? Will your horse shy if he passes too close to the concession stand and hears the pots and pans rattle? Can you ride closer to the inside of the arena to avoid spooking him? When you stop to enter a back-up, where does your horse need

The show committee works long and hard to put on a good show—not always in the best of weather. Here they give the course a last-minute check. You, too, may want to walk the course before your class.

to be to set up the best? Will he side-pass to put you closer to the gate, or must you ride in a straight line to meet the gate correctly? Know your horse and how he works the best and plan your trip accordingly.

HIGHLIGHT WHAT YOUR HORSE DOES BEST

Try to highlight what your horse does best. If he is unflappable and most of the horses before you have spooked at one area of the arena, ride specifically into that area of the arena to show off your horse's good nature. Always stay within the limits of the pattern. Where does your horse shine? Stress his good points and minimize his weak areas. Ride straight lines unless the pattern calls for a curved line. A horse that wanders or doesn't track in a straight line does not look polished.

HANDLING NO-SCORES AND DISQUALIFICATION

A "no-score" on an obstacle is not a disqualification from the entire course. A no-score results from missing or not attempting an obstacle, failure to complete an obstacle, failure to be in the correct gait or correct lead, or doing the obstacle differently than is designated by the pattern.

A disqualification from the class results from doing the obstacles in a different order than designated by the pattern, using illegal equipment, willful abuse of the horse, a major disobedience of the horse such as rearing, or from excessively schooling your horse in the ring. Use of more than one finger between the reins (when riding one-handed) is cause for disqualification. So is obviously cueing a horse to drop his head to "look" at an obstacle.

If you receive a no-score on an obstacle, ride the balance of the pattern to the best of your ability and try to make up points. If you disqualify for some reason, use your mistake to help you in the future. If you benefit from your mistakes, they were worth making.

KNOW THE RULES

It is important that you know the rules of the association in which you plan to show. Read them carefully to see what is and what is not allowed. Watch a few horses ahead of you ride the pattern. Look for obstacles that seem troublesome. Think of your horse and of how you might help him on that obstacle. Picture him doing it correctly. Ride with confidence, not trepidation or fear. If your horse feels hesitation on your part, chances are he will also hesitate over the obstacle.

Watch the riders before you to see how the course rides. If watching the other riders makes you nervous or leaves you feeling as if your horse will never maneuver through the pattern as cleanly, watch a class in which you are not competing. See if you can gain insight into the best way to approach or negotiate through an obstacle. Work on gaining more confidence in yourself and your horse. Rather than getting nervous about riding the pattern (and what may or may not go wrong), re-focus your energy on how to ride each obstacle. Block out the sights and sounds of the arena and focus only on how to guide your horse so that he can best negotiate that obstacle. Feel what your horse is doing. Is he traveling straight? Are you lined up correctly with the obstacle? Is his attention on you? Are his feet placed correctly?

If you enter the arena worrying about what others will think, you set yourself up for problems. Forget the audience, the noise, the other horses. Concentrate solely on getting the maximum performance from your horse. Use your aids—legs, seat, weight and hands—without over-cueing to guide your horse cleanly through each obstacle. If your horse bumps a pole, don't dwell on it. Focus on doing the next obstacle. If your horse feels your intense concentration, chances are that he will concentrate, too. If he feels you worry, he'll worry too.

Think positively to set yourself up for success. I have repeated this over and over in hopes that it will stick in your mind. When a horse is not behaving up to your expectations, focus on how to turn the situation to your benefit. Don't just let things happen, make them happen. Ride to the best of your ability. Ride your horse to the best of his ability. If he's weak on an obstacle at home, don't expect him to miraculously come through at a show. Ride the obstacle the best you can, then continue to school your horse at home. Take a lesson or ask a trainer for help. It will come in time. Don't dwell on the negatives.

Watch your attitude! Do you fall apart if your horse refuses an obstacle? (Remember—it's only one obstacle.) While you will lose points, or possibly receive a no-score, you have the remaining obstacles on which to gain points. Rather than let one obstacle upset you, let that obstacle encourage you to try harder on the balance of the obstacles. Try to gain back the points you lost. Think, "How can I do this better?" instead of "My horse is dumb." Remember, you are the trainer. The horse learns what you teach him.

USE A CUE TO RE-FOCUS YOUR HORSE

You should have a specific cue in place to regain your horse's attention if it wanders. I lift my reins (up towards the sky) and lightly bump them once or twice. From earlier training, the horse knows to softly flex at the poll and give his face. You'll feel his jaw dip back slightly towards his neck. There should be no resistance transmitted through the reins. When a horse gives you his face (or his mouth), he gives you his mind. Flexing in response to a light lift and bump on the reins should re-focus his attention on you. Lifting both reins upwards lifts the horse's shoulders. Sometimes when a horse tries to evade an obstacle, he will drop a shoulder on one side or the other and try to duck out to one side. Lifting both reins causes him to re-balance. Lifting the reins becomes a signal that says, "Hey! Pay attention to me. Straighten up. Re-balance your body and follow your nose until I ask you to do otherwise."

If he didn't immediately heed your cue to re-focus, you will feel resistance in his mouth as you bump the reins. Rather than get a correct soft and giving feeling, you will have to pull on the reins to get any response.

Sometimes, what feels "off" is noticeable only to you. If you remain alert to the slightest sign of evasion on your horse's part, often you can fix it and only you will be the wiser.

Older riders enjoy trail, too. If the horse stops correctly next to the barrel, this rider will get a Halloween treat from the pumpkin. It can be fun to ride in trail class.

at this point in time? Know the distances for jog-overs and lope-overs and other obstacles that will show him to his best ability. Know how long it takes for him to respond to a given cue. Does he lope right off when you apply the cue? Or is he a little sluggish? Does he need more time to prepare to lope? Only you know what your horse requires. Learn how your horse rides each obstacle the best. Know when he will let you help him and when he maneuvers best on his own. Practice and polish, polish and practice, until you know your horse inside and out. Then ride him the same way through the class.

KNOW YOUR HORSE

You must know the correct way of going for your horse at the walk, jog, and lope. Are his gaits consistent and rhythmical? Are his departures, transitions, and halts perfect for him

SMILE!

Never let your facial expressions give a clue to what your horse is doing unless it's a big, confident smile. Your facial expressions and attitude should shout (non-verbally), "This is fun! My

Mr. McAllister judging the Harwinton Fair in Connecticut. This was a Halloween course with spooky goblins added to some of the obstacles.

horse is the best! I'm enjoying this class." Whether your horse is being good or bad, you want the judge to think that you are enjoying yourself. A judge will remember a contestant that has a bad attitude. Show with a happy, smiling face that shows a pleasant attitude, even if it feels like your horse is falling apart. Remember, one bad obstacle won't disqualify you from the class. Ride the rest of the course to the best of your ability. If your horse is having a bad day, chalk it up to experience. The judge understands that horses have good days and bad days, yet he must judge what is presented to him in this class on this day.

WHAT THE JUDGE LOOKS FOR

A judge looks at your horse's attitude, his willingness, and his way of going. He looks for a good attitude, and the partnership between you and your horse. He looks at the way you control your horse. He looks at the way you and your horse maneuver through an obstacle as a team. Are your cues soft and subtle? Your corrections a gentle reminder? Or do you yank, jerk, or spur? Not only does that look bad to the judge, it is not the impression that you want to give to the spectators, to the youth riders, or to fellow exhibitors. The judge is looking for a polished, professional performance from a horse that knows his job and a rider that allows the horse to show to the best of his ability. He looks for a horse that matches the rider in personality. A strong horse with a timid rider is not a good match. This will show when you negotiate the pattern. He looks for a horse that compliments the rider's size. A tiny rider looks out of place on a big horse and vice versa. He wants to see if your tack is neat and clean, giving the appearance that you care about doing well. Be sure all straps and buckles are in their correct place with no loose ends hanging to distract his attention as you negotiate the obstacles. Be sure your blanket is large enough for your saddle and that it hangs equally below the skirt of the saddle on either side. Colors that compliment your horse are also part of a winning picture.

When practicing, these clothes are acceptable.

HAVE YOU DRESSED APPROPRIATELY

A judge does not judge you on the clothes that you wear. He looks for a neatly attired exhibitor with a well-trained horse that negotiates the obstacles cleanly and professionally. The best clothes you can buy will not improve your horse's way of going, or his style over obstacles. On the other hand, a "dressed-for-success" look with the current style clothes is the image that you want. Clothes give an image of success. Your smile gives the appearance of confidence, and your horse shows that you have done the homework to perform professionally.

THE FINISHED PRODUCT

Making and "finishing" a trail horse is a long, slow process. It takes a little bit of skill and a lot of patience. You must have the ability to feel when your horse is right (so you leave him alone) and when your horse is wrong (so you correct him). On the up side, once a horse is trained for trail, you will have the ability to put your horse anywhere you want him. Even if you never show, riding a well-trained trail horse is like driving a sports car. You can go in and out of places that others would fear to go. And, if you trained

Same horse, same rider, many miles of conditioning later, dressed for success! Jerrie Monroe on Sunny.

the horse yourself, you'll feel like you created a masterpiece! Which, in fact, you have: a horse that obeys your every command, whether to go forward, backwards, sideways, left, right, over, through, or around an obstacle. What more could anyone ask?

Riding a well-trained trail horse is like driving a sports car. You can put him anywhere you want him. If you trained him yourself, you'll feel like you created a masterpiece! Photo © Dusty Perin.

PATTERNS

THINK OF A TRAIL PATTERN as a series of separate obstacles that are judged one by one. The score also includes gaits and way of going between obstacles. These separate obstacle scores are then tallied for a total score.

The AQHA uses a system of scoring that is similar to how reining horses are scored. Each horse enters the arena with a score of 70 which denotes an average performance. Each obstacle receives an obstacle score that is either added or subtracted from the beginning 70 according to how the horse performs. For example, on one obstacle you may score a plus one, which then gives you a 71, but on the next obstacle you may receive a minus one and one-half, bringing your score to 69 1/2, and so on. In addition, certain penalty points are deducted. These may include, but are not limited to, ticking a pole, minus one-half point. Stepping on a pole, 1 point deduction. Break of gait at a walk or jog for two strides or less, 1 point penalty. Break of gait at a walk or jog for more than two strides is a 3 point penalty. Dropping a slicker or other object that is to be carried, or a first refusal or balking at an obstacle is a 5 point penalty. Read your rule book to find how your association judges the class.

Every judge has an ideal for each maneuver in his head and he judges the horse against that visualized ideal. That is why, if three people are judging a class, they can place a particular horse in three different positions even though he performed the same pattern in the exact same way. Each judge's idea of perfection is different. When you enter a class, you pay for a judge's opinion on a given day. You compete against other contestants whose performance may or may not, in your mind, be better than yours. However, it is the judge's opinion that counts, and he or she decides what is ideal and scores each maneuver accordingly. Because you are scored on each maneuver, having one bad obstacle should not affect the way you ride the balance of the pattern. Take a deep breath, gather your thoughts, and put that obstacle completely out of your mind. You can gain points on the rest of the obstacles and still do well, depending on how your competitors perform. Make it your goal to perform each obstacle to the best of your ability.

GATHER TRAIL OBSTACLES

Collect equipment and articles that you can use to make trail patterns at home. Having a variety of obstacles

A cone back-up. To perform this correctly, you would back in a half-circle around the cone beside the horse's right hind foot and exit between the two cones nearest his front feet.

ed. A raised bridge made of sturdy lumber is also a good investment. You can make a mailbox by tacking a small box on a jump standard or on a pole on your arena. A sheet of plastic can substitute for a slicker. Your horse will never know the difference. If it blows in the wind and crinkles like a slicker, it will be all the same to him. You can make a practice water obstacle simply by filling a depression with water, or you can build a box and line the bottom with plastic to hold the water. If you see an obstacle at a show that you like, see if you can create one that is similar. If your horse has a problem with a specific obstacle, recreate that obstacle at home so that you can practice. Trail obstacles are limited only by your imagination.

and the material to create new and varied obstacles will expose your horse to things he might face at a show. This will help your horse when it comes time to show. Practicing obstacles at home allows you to fine-tune cues. You learn to achieve the most precise movements possible over the obstacles. Just don't drill over and over on any one obstacle. Your horse will grow to hate that obstacle and will perform it worse, rather than better. Variety is one of the secrets to keeping your horse's interest high.

You will need as many poles as you can afford. If you can't buy poles, small trees that have a long, straight, slender look will work. Cut the branches off, paint them white or striped with other colors, and use them as poles. Twenty poles is a good number to start. Look for flower pots and potted shrubs to give your course color and variety. A sheet of plywood makes a good starting bridge. Leave one side plain and paint the other side white. Flip it from side to side as need-

SAMPLE PATTERNS

Some sample trail patterns follow, starting with the easiest and ending with more complicated patterns such as you will find at a large breed show. Practice the easy courses until your horse gains confidence in the maneuvers. Then begin to add a degree of difficulty. Once your horse can master the courses listed here, be creative and move the obstacles around to create new patterns. Ride the courses forward and then backwards, if the obstacles are set in a way that allows you to do so. Approach the obstacles from a different direction. Be creative. Keep it interesting.

Happy trails!

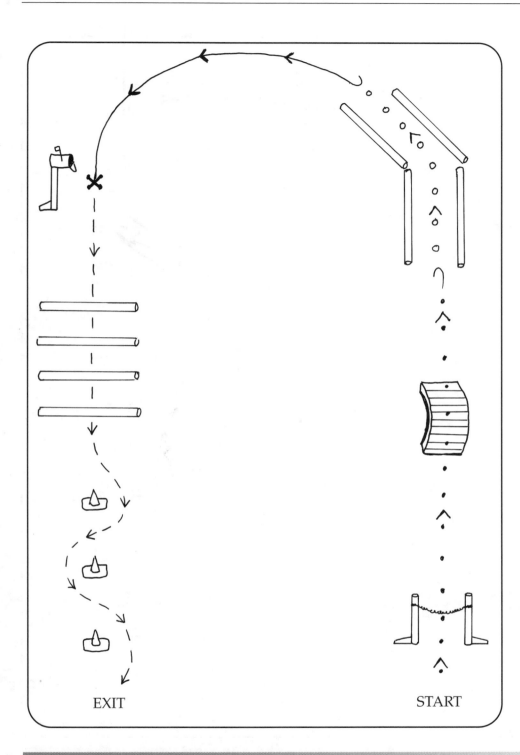

EXIT   START

PATTERN 1

1. Gate
2. Walk over bridge
3. Back through "L"
4. Lope, left lead to mailbox
5. Show mail
6. Jog over poles
7. Jog and serpentine through cones.

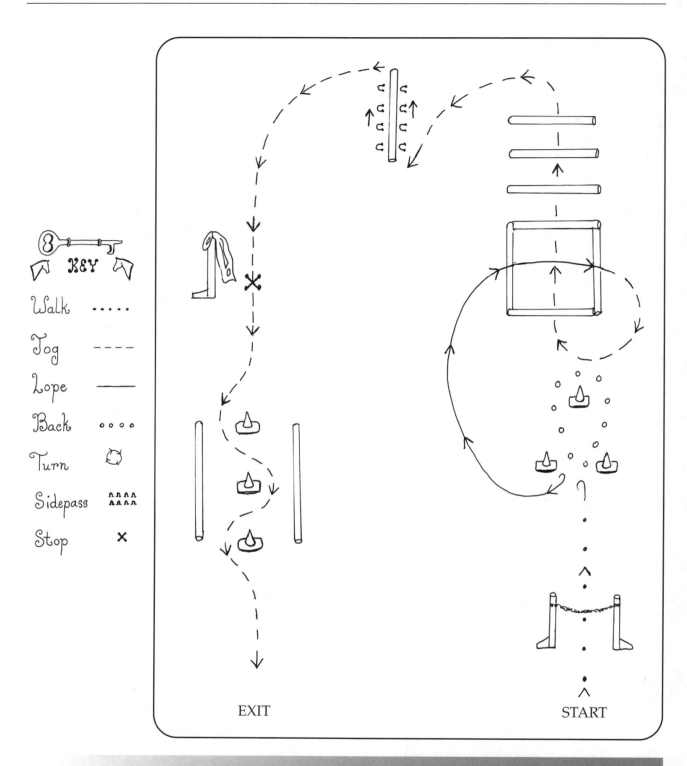

PATTERN 2

1. Gate
2. Back around cones
3. Lope, right lead, through box
4. Jog through box and poles
5. Side pass to right
6. Jog to Slicker
7. Jog and serpentine cones

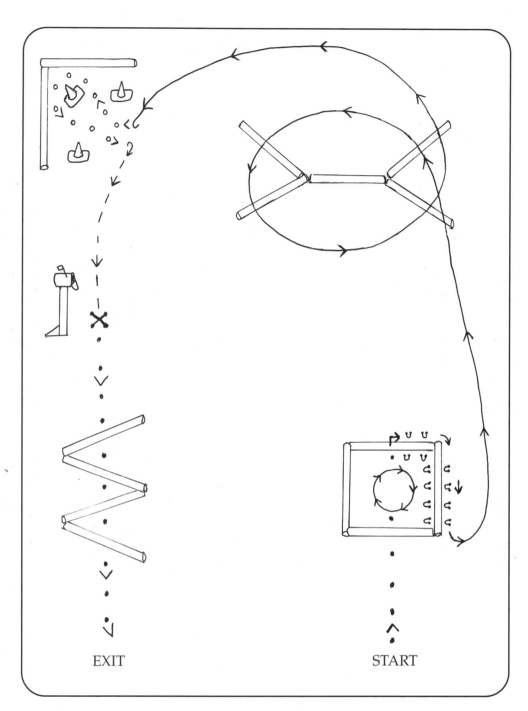

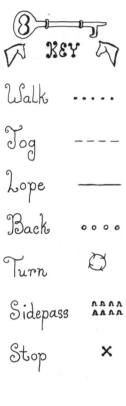

PATTERN 3

1. Walk into box and do a 360
2. Step 1/2 way out of box and sidepass (right) the "L"
3. Lope the poles, left lead
4. Back around cones, staying inside the guide poles
5. Jog to mail box, remove mail, show to judge, replace
6. Walk over poles

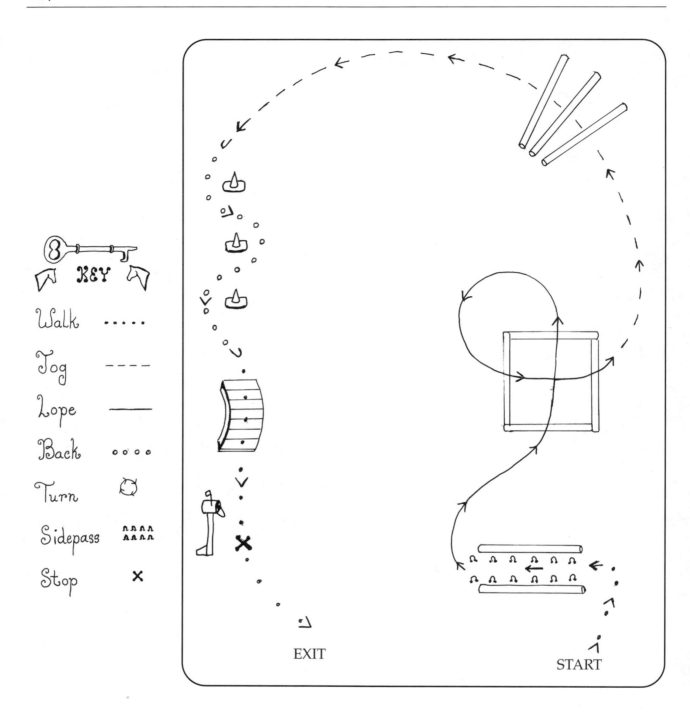

PATTERN 4

1. Open arena gate to enter
   Side pass left, staying between the poles
2. Lope the box. Tip: Slightly angle your horse to the
   right, hesitate briefly (30 seconds) to let him settle,
   then ask for a left lead lope
3. Jog over poles
4. Back through cones
5. Walk over bridge
6. Open mailbox and show mail to judge.

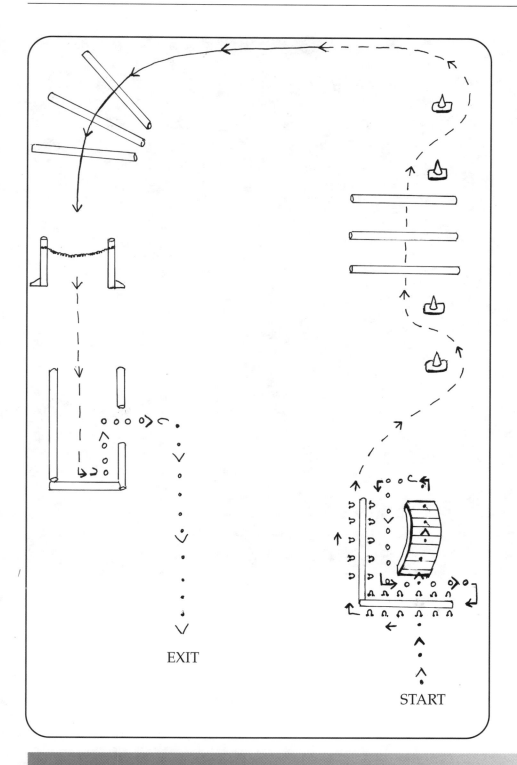

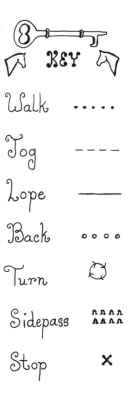

EXIT

START

PATTERN 5

1. Walk over bridge
2. Back through "L"
3. Side pass (left)
4. Jog through cones and over poles
5. Lope over poles
6. Work Gate
7. Jog into chute stop, and back out as shown
8. Walk and exit

GLOSSARY

Agility. The ability to maneuver easily over and across obstacles.

Artificial aids. Spurs, martingales, or a crop which may be used temporarily but try not to depend on them to cue your horse. Teach your horse to respond to the natural aids, or cues.

Athletic. An athletic horse is supple and flexible and able to maneuver skillfully, much like a human athlete.

Between the bridle. The horse's head is looking straight forward, thus "between the bridle."

Cadence of gait. The rhythm of a horse's gait should be consistent. A walk is a four-beat gait, one, two, three, four. A jog is a two-beat gait, one, two, one, two. A lope is a three-beat gait, one, two, three, one, two, three.

Cues. The tools we use—hands, legs, and weight or seat aids—to give a horse directions.

Flex at the poll. A horse must flex at the poll in response to light rein pressure. When a horse flexes at the poll, he is said to give you his face, indicating that he is willing to listen to your cues. An untrained or evasive horse will often fight the bit and raise his head in the air, making it difficult, if not impossible, to cue him with the reins.

Frame. When a horse is in a frame, he flexes at the poll and holds his head in a vertical position. His back is up and rounded, and he is driving from behind. This is pretty to look at, and the horse is is able to use his body to his maximum potential.

Hips. Hindquarters or rear of the horse.

Hold the horse's head between your hands. Usually done with a rein in each hand. Use your reins to keep his nose pointing straight ahead. If he turns his head to the left, use your right direct rein to straighten his head and vice versa.

Hoof angles that don't match. The angle of both the front hooves should match. The hoof angle should match the pastern angle, which should match the shoulder angle.

Long toe, no heel. This can create unsoundness in a horse. It is simply what it says. The toe of the hoof is too long making it hard for a horse to break over correctly, and the heel is too short, thus no heel to support his weight.

Move flat. A horse that moves flat moves his front legs as an extension of the shoulder. He does not have excessive knee action or lift his knees high like a Hackney pony. He is a good moving horse.

Move the horse's head, hip, shoulders. You move the horse's head and shoulders with your reins, and the hips and hind end with your legs. You must be able to place the various parts of your horse's body to negotiate the obstacles.

Natural talent. A horse is born with natural talent. It is our job as trainers to find what that natural talent is best suited for.

Shoulder angle. The angle from the withers to the point of the shoulder. A horse's shoulder angle determines the length of his stride. He can only extend his leg to the extent that his shoulder angle allows. A very straight shoulder and resulting straight pastern angle makes the horse uncomfortable as he hits the ground too hard. He has no pastern angulation to absorb the shock.

Sidepass. The horse crosses his left leg over his right leg to move right, or vice versa. The body remains straight as the horse travels sideways.

Slow legged. A horse that naturally moves his legs slowly. Therefore, his whole body will move slowly.

Soft and willing. A horse that is soft and willing does not show signs of evasion or resentment. He wants to please and he obeys light, barely visible, cues.

Straight pastern. A straight pastern (matches a straight shoulder) has no angulation to absorb shock, thus giving you a rough ride.

Toe in. Points the toes in rather than straight ahead. This horse will not move as well as a horse that is straight and correct.

Toe out. The opposite of the above. This horse will often interfere or bump his opposite leg as he moves.

Track straight. The legs follow a straight line, neither winging or paddling or moving to the side.

About The Author

The author owns and trains at Silver Creek Farm in Athens, Texas, where she also stands a black and white Paint stallion, SC Splashsrobinsboy. She starts colts, trains and shows halter horses, pleasure and trail horses, hunters and jumpers, and All-Around horses.

May you always ride a good horse! The author, Laurie Truskauskas, aboard SC Splashsrobinsboy.

Truskauskas has written over one hundred articles for *Western Horseman, Quarter Horse Journal, Horse and Horseman, The Western Horse, The Paint Horse Journal, The Pinto Horse magazine, Palomino magazine,* and other regional papers. This is her sixth book on horse training.

Laurie apprenticed with Joe Ferro, one of the men responsible for starting the American Quarter Horse Association in 1942. Joe's son, Roy Ferro, won the first National Reining Horse Association Futurity. While with Joe, Laurie learned about starting colts, breeding and foaling. With his encouragement, she put on paper their combined knowledge in hopes of helping others who search for knowledge about training the horse. *Training the Two-Year-Old Colt* is her first book, and each succeeding book gives insight into a new topic.

She has judged local and open shows and has given clinics to 4-H and other clubs. She has shown at the Congress and finds the entire experience—from judging youth to showing top quality horses—to be truly rewarding. Perhaps her greatest thrill is watching an owner's face when a horse she has trained does well for the owner in the ring.

YOU'LL WANT TO READ THESE, TOO . . .

Understanding Showmanship (Equi-Skills Series)

Laurie Truskauskas

Learn the fine art of presenting a winning picture in the Showmanship Classes. Includes key things to consider when selecting a horse for showmanship, six basic patterns you can learn, how to put the winning touches into grooming, and more.
Softcover, ISBN 1-57779-030-8

The ABC's of Showmanship
Teach the Showmanship Maneuvers
Step by Step

Laurie Truskauskas

Pocket-sized companion to Understanding Showmanship gives concise instructions on patterns and showmanship exercises.
An Alpine Arena Handbook
Comb binding, ISBN 1-57779-031-6

Horse Anatomy, A Coloring Atlas

Robert Kainer, DVM and Thomas McCracken, MS

This unique learning tool has eighty-one detailed drawings of all parts of the horse accompanied by descriptions and common problems affecting that portion of the anatomy. The reader is invited to color in as you read to enjoy an almost "hands-on" experience. Selected as reference material for National 4-H Horse Bowl and Hippology competition.
Wire bound, Softcover ISBN 1-57779-021-9

Mental Equitation

James Arrigon

The first book to provide a proven, systematic program of riding based on the theories of classical horsemanship. Equally applicable for western and English riders. The author is a University equitation instructor and coach of a successful collegiate equestrian team.
Hardcover, ISBN 1-57779-010-3

Almost a Whisper

Sam Powell

Learn to communicate effectively and safely with your horse and how his instincts as a herd and a prey animal affect how you should handle and train him. Powell is a master horseman and shares his years of experience and observation in a manner anyone can understand and use. Covers colt starting, trailer loading, problem solving and more.
Hardcover, ISBN 1-57779-026-X

Training the Two-Year-Old Colt

Laurie Truskauskas

With this book as your guide you can start your first horse with confidence. Start by teaching your weanling basic manners and continue step by step through your two-year-old's first thirty days under saddle and beyond. Truskauskas is a trainer and exhibitor of western pleasure and reining horses who learned her trade under the skillful guidance of trainer Joe Ferro of Quarter Horse fame.
Hardcover, ISBN 1-57779-004-9

How to Use Leg Wraps, Bandages & Boots

Sue A. Allen

The only book to explain all types of wraps, boots and bandages, and how and when to use them. Also covers preventative care and treatment for leg injuries and strains. Allen is a riding instructor and often gives clinics on equine leg care.
Softcover, ISBN 0-931866-72-3

COMING SOON IN THE EQUI-SKILLS SERIES

Finishing the Western Horse

Safe Trail Riding

Experiences Along the Way (Training)

These and other fine Alpine titles are available at your local bookseller or you may order direct from the publisher at 1-800-777-7257 or writing to Alpine Publications, 225 S. Madison Ave., Loveland, CO 80537.

For the latest information and prices visit our website: www.AlpinePub.com.